More Advance Praise for *The Key to the C-Suite*

"Nick provides a well-thought-out, metric-driven analysis of how C-level executives make decisions that get beyond the standard acronym-driven methodologies that sales people are normally taught."
 —GARTH MOULTON, Senior Director of Community, Salesforce.com,
  and co-founder, Jigsaw

"Michael pushes the value creation envelope further by helping to create a 'financial pain-gain model' to help salespeople mediate meaningful discussions with CXOs."
 —VICTOR ANTONIO, Sales Influence

"An easy-to-read, demystifying explanation of how to create tools necessary to interact, communicate with, and sell to C-Suite executives. *The Key to the C-Suite* opens the door to successfully selling to top executives."
 —JOE BOLIAN, President , Taxography, Inc.

"This book will take consultative selling to a totally new level for those organizations that incorporate the major C-Suite metrics in their selling processes. Following the book's systematic approach will give sales professionals the knowledge and tools they need to be viewed as business consultants, and not 'tell and sell' vendors, by their prospective buyers."
 —BOB KANTIN, President, SalesProposals.com

"Finally, a credible way to measure the financial impact on an organization's top and bottom line. Thank you, Michael Nick!"
 —GURU GANESHA, Sandler Training, the "Sales Guru for the High Tech Industry"

"In the current economic environment, buying decisions are made at the C-level, forcing sales professionals to speak a different language and adopt better tools in order to survive. *The Key to the C-Suite* simplifies the C-level vernacular, provides a solid education of strategic buying, and illustrates how to tie value to financial impact by moving beyond an ROI sales model."
 —HARRY DEAN BILLIPS, Vice President, Sales and Marketing, Tax Compliance, Inc.

The
KEY
— *to the* —
C-SUITE

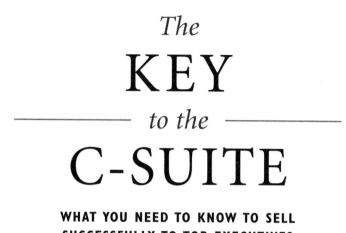

The

KEY

to the

C-SUITE

**WHAT YOU NEED TO KNOW TO SELL
SUCCESSFULLY TO TOP EXECUTIVES**

MICHAEL J. NICK

AMACOM

AMERICAN MANAGEMENT ASSOCIATION

New York • Atlanta • Brussels • Chicago • Mexico City • San Francisco
Shanghai • Tokyo • Toronto • Washington, D.C.

This publication is designed to provide accurate and authoritative information in regard to the subject matter covered. It is sold with the understanding that the publisher is not engaged in rendering legal, accounting, or other professional service. If legal advice or other expert assistance is required, the services of a competent professional person should be sought.

Library of Congress Cataloging-in-Publication Data

Nick, Michael J.
    The key to the C-suite : what you need to know to sell successfully to top executives / Michael J. Nick.
        p. cm.
    Includes index.
    ISBN-13: 978-0-8144-1730-0
    ISBN-10: 0-8144-1730-2
    1. Selling. 2. Sales management. 3. Executives. 4. Consumer behavior. I. Title.
    HF5438.25.N523 2011
    658.85--dc22   2011007609

About AMA

American Management Association (www.amanet.org) is a world leader in talent development, advancing the skills of individuals to drive business success. Our mission is to support the goals of individuals and organizations through a complete range of products and services, including classroom and virtual seminars, webcasts, webinars, podcasts, conferences, corporate and government solutions, business books and research. AMA's approach to improving performance combines experiential learning—learning through doing—with opportunities for ongoing professional growth at every step of one's career journey.

Printing number
10 9 8 7 6 5 4 3 2 1

CONTENTS

FOREWORD

What does it take to capture and keep the attention of today's crazy-busy executives? Perhaps you're still under the illusion that they're interested in your products, services, or solutions.

If so, you're in for a rude awakening. In fact, your offering is so irrelevant that even talking about it in early meetings with C-level executives is a serious breach of etiquette. The result? You immediately lose credibility, and they see you as one more lightweight, self-serving salesperson. Potential opportunities come to a screeching halt.

I've seen this happen repeatedly. Most salespeople simply don't know what it takes to engage senior executives in a peer-to-peer conversation. They lack the business acumen and customer insight to understand the true value of their offering. Worse yet, because their companies fail to provide this information, many salespeople don't even know what they're missing.

But what you don't know can hurt you—badly. It can cripple your sales efforts and make you work ten times harder to reach your quota. I've been in those situations, and I'm sure you have, too. It's no fun to be continually scrambling to meet your numbers.

That's why *The Key to the C-Suite* is an essential tool that belongs on every salesperson's desk. In today's economy, virtually all decisions are being scrutinized to determine whether they'll contribute value to the company's bottom line. And you need to be the one who tells senior executives what your offering specifically means for them because they're often too busy to figure it out on their own.

In this book, Michael Nick has laid out a detailed blueprint for clearly articulating your business case in a manner that's highly appealing to C-Suite executives. First, you learn their language. Then, you get inside your product or service, offering to figure out its true contribution to their business objectives.

Step by step, you're led through exactly what you need to do to get your prospects to consider making a change. Once you learn how to do this, you'll become an unstoppable force. Why? Because frazzled prospects don't have enough time to think and strategize on how to improve their business.

They're looking for trusted resources that have their best interests in mind. They want to work with people who bring them ideas and insights on how to achieve their objectives. They'll definitely pay attention when you contact them with an idea on how to "increase the average order size on your web site by up to 14 percent" or how to significantly "reduce time to revenue on new product launches."

That's the kind of specific offering that gets them drooling. They'll ask you in to meet with them. They'll want to learn how you did this for others. They'll invite their colleagues to meet with you as well.

Suddenly the status quo is no longer acceptable. It's time to seriously consider doing something different. You're now in the driver's seat—leading the change initiative. And it all started because you knew how to build a strong business case when talking to C-Suite executives.

—**Jill Konrath,** author of *SNAP Selling* and *Selling to Big Companies*

ACKNOWLEDGMENTS

For my mother, Nicki, who passed away this year: I will miss you so much.

My son, Jonathan—I am so proud of the man you are turning into. I will miss you dearly when you leave for college. I love you, son.

My daughter, Jessica—I am so proud of all the things you have accomplished at such a young age. Honey, keep dancing like nobody is watching. I love you.

Michelle—you are the love of my life. Thank you for your patience and encouragement.

Jill Konrath—thank you for writing the foreword, and thank you for being a great friend.

Ken Edmundson, my mentor—thank you for driving me to succeed. Your talks mean more to me than you will ever know.

John Willig, my agent—thank you for getting this project off the ground.

Bob Nirkind, my editor—thank you for believing in this project and being patient with the editing process.

The editing staff at AMACOM—thank you, I know this wasn't easy.

Tom Hayes, my friend, my colleague, and my sounding board—your thoughts and ideas are always appreciated.

Bob Kantin, my friend—thank you for the help putting this book together. Using the concepts in this book, maybe Johnny can sell.

I would also like to thank my friend Jim Norton, Harvey Shovers, Dave Hunkele, Bryan Flanagan, Jill Konrath, Sharon Drew Morgan, Michael Bosworth, Ron Marks, Joanne Black, Michael Norton, Keith Rosen, Ken Edmundson, Michael Drake, Steve Szamocki, and Charlie Gibbons for participating in "What they don't teach you in sales training."

The
KEY
to the
C-SUITE

INTRODUCTION

Several years ago, Kurt M. Koenig and I published a book called ROI Selling (Kaplan Publishing, 2004), in which we covered in detail how to create sales tools focused around return on investment (ROI). Back then, ROI was a key tool that was required in most complex sales environments. We had just come out of the dot-com era, and there was a lot of skepticism about the value that companies could offer. Most organizations were forced to create some sort of sales tool that performed complex math projecting positive ROI. This trend lasted for several years until the economy took another turn for the worse in 2008.

ROI models are still used today in many sales opportunities, with limited success. However, in the past few years, we have seen economic changes like never before. Budgets have become even more stringent, decisions to buy any asset have been put off indefinitely, and important purchasing decisions have been moved up the ladder into the C-Suite. My research indicates that most major buying decisions will now include a financial executive on the team. Once again we are faced with a new era of selling that will require better sales tools and a new approach. This book is about creating the tools you will need if you are to interact with, communicate with, and sell to C-Suite executives.

The Key to the C-Suite introduces many new concepts for selling to senior executives. These concepts will help you better understand how to match your value proposition to your prospects' desire and financial ability to buy from you. This process requires that you learn about the financial impact your products and services will have on a prospect's financial status.

After reading this book, you will be able to recognize key information about your prospects that will help you determine their financial stability. In addition, we identify a series of financial metrics that C-level executives use to make strategic buying decisions. *The Key to the C-Suite* will teach you how to discuss the value of your product or service as it relates to these defined financial metrics. Conveying your value to a prospect must begin the first time you meet. If you are able to identify your prospect's issues, pains, and goals and articulate your value as it relates to the impact on the prospect's most widely used financial metrics, then you are one step closer to communicating with the C-Suite at a different level from your competition.

The first eight chapters each cover a concept that ultimately is used in building sales tools, leading up to the development of your C-Suite business case. As you move from chapter to chapter, you will realize the importance of learning the concepts in one chapter before moving on to the next. These chapters are laid out to explain the issue, discuss the solutions, provide examples, and then summarize the ideas for you to use as you build your own sales tools.

In Chapter 9, we put our concepts to the test in the real world. We asked some of the best sales trainers, customers, and colleagues to answer one simple question: "What is it that you were not taught in sales training?" (In other words, what did you have to learn on your own?) Bryan Flanagan, Mike Bosworth, Jill Konrath, Keith Rosen, and others tell us what they had to learn on their own. By applying the principles presented in *The Key to the C-Suite* to their comments, we give you some real-world understanding of how to use the concepts you've learned throughout the book.

Our research for this book extends over the past five years and includes participation from dozens of companies worldwide. We interviewed hundreds of sales professionals, midlevel managers, and C-level executives from organizations like Hewlett-Packard, Rockwell Automation, TSYS, Fiserv, S1, GE, and Emerson Process Controls to develop the concepts and principles used throughout the book.

Remember, work through each chapter, mastering one chapter at a time, and you will soon be in the C-Suite successfully selling your products and services.

THE C-SUITE EFFECT

C-level executives spend the majority of their time focusing on strategic objectives. Their primary objective overall, however, is to sell more products and services and make their companies as profitable as possible. Basic profit is determined by how much you sell in comparison to the cost of what you buy. When C-level executives make major buying decisions, they take into account the cost to purchase and its effect on a set of simple metrics that they use to help them determine such things as when to buy, the method of payment, and the value to the company relative to the amount spent. In addition, they will often look into the effect that this purchase will have on their financial statements and annual reports.

Communicating with these decision makers (C-level executives) requires a different set of sales tools and selling skills, and a basic knowledge of their vernacular. In this chapter, we reveal to you the language that C-level executives live by, the metrics they use in making buying decisions, and how to establish a foundation for building the tools necessary to succeed when selling to the C-Suite.

> **The C-Suite Effect:** *C-level executives make buying decisions based on the strategic effect that a purchase will have on a set of key financial metrics or levers.*

For example, let's begin with a prospect's chief financial officer (CFO). The CFO is the originator of much of the information that is used to make most buying decisions in every organization. The CFO keeps all of this information in places where it can be used for the analysis of such things as what to buy and when to make a buying decision.

Here is a revelation for you: *ROI is no longer the key metric that the CFO really cares about in the buying decision process.*

The basic problem with ROI is that it is typically calculated (estimated) before purchase and implementation, but rarely calculated (proven) after delivery. In addition, even when you do return to measure the value delivered, it is usually too late to make a move to correct issues that arose over the course of the project implementation.

This lack of measurement after implementation renders ROI calculations a useless tool for today's sales professionals to rely on in the sales process. In addition, there are some instances in which ROI is not achieved for several years. A more effective approach is to discuss your prospect's issues, pains, and goals as they relate to your product's value and its effect on the key financial metrics that CFOs use to understand their company's financial stability and make informed financial buying decisions—in other words, the C-Suite effect.

MAJOR C-SUITE METRICS

There are more than 20 metrics that CFOs may use to monitor the financial health of their organization and calculate or track spending. We are going to focus on 10 of the most popular metrics that are used in various ways to evaluate most strategic buying decisions within a corporation. If you have a basic understanding of what each metric means and its impact on the buying decision, then you have achieved the first step in effectively moving beyond selling using ROI, TCO (total cost of ownership), or other financial models.

In this section we will identify 10 of the major C-Suite metrics (financial levers) followed by their definition and a breakdown of their calculation. (Tip: Keep this list close to you for future reference.) These metrics are:

1. Return on assets (ROA)

2. Return on equity (ROE)

3. Earnings

4. Operating costs

5. Net and gross profit margin

6. Payroll as a percentage of sales

7. Sales per employee

8. Debt-to-equity ratio

9. Earnings before interest, taxes, depreciation, and amortization (EBITDA) margin

10. Days' sales outstanding (DSO)

Return on Assets (ROA)

ROA is an indicator of how profitable a company is relative to its total assets. The assets of a company are supported by both debt and equity. The ROA percentage gives investors an idea of how effectively the company is converting the money that it has to invest into net income. It is most effective to compare the current ROA to the previous year's ROA. The higher the ROA percentage, the better, because a higher ROA means that the company is earning more money on less investment. For example, if one company has a net income of $10 million and total assets of $50 million, its ROA is 20 percent ($50 million/$10 million); however, if another company earns the same amount but has total assets of $100 million, it has an ROA of 10 percent. Based on this example, the first company is better at converting its investment into profit. Calculation:

$$ROA = Net\ Income \div Total\ Assets$$

Return on Equity (ROE)

Sometimes called "return on net worth," *ROE* measures a corporation's profitability by revealing how much profit it generates with the money that shareholders have invested. Displayed as a percentage, ROE is useful for comparing the profitability of a company to that of other firms in the same industry. Calculation:

$$\text{ROE} = \text{Net Income} \div \text{Shareholders' Equity}$$

Earnings

Earnings are revenues minus cost of sales, operating expenses, and taxes over a given period of time. Calculation:

$$\text{Earnings} = \text{Revenues} - (\text{Operating Expenses} + \text{Taxes})$$

Operating Costs

Operating costs are the day-to-day expenses incurred in running a business. For example, the cost of sales and administrative costs are considered to be operating costs. Production costs are not considered operating costs.

Net and Gross Profit Margin

Net profit margin is the bottom line—the amount that is left after every other expense is taken out. *Gross profit margin* is revenue minus what it costs to make the product. Calculations:

$$\text{Net Profit Margin} = \text{Total Revenue} - \text{Total Expense}$$

$$\text{Gross Profit Margin} = (\text{Sales} - \text{Costs Directly Related to Those Sales})$$

Payroll as a Percentage of Sales

This simple calculation is important because our research indicates that much of the value delivered by organizations comes from a reduction in labor cost. The average U.S. corporation keeps this figure at around 20 to 23 percent, depending upon the market that the corporation serves. Calculation:

Payroll as a Percentage of Sales = Total Payroll Expense ÷ Total Revenue

Sales per Employee

Once again, this metric is one of the most affected when calculating value delivered. If your product or service increases revenue or reduces labor cost, it will positively affect this metric. Calculation:

Sales per Employee = Total Sales ÷ Total Payroll Expense

Debt-to-Equity Ratio

This ratio is used as a relative measure of debt—in other words, what a company owes in relation to what it owns. The two components in the calculation—i.e., total liabilities and total equity—come from the balance sheet. Calculation:

Debt-to-Equity Ratio = Total Liabilities ÷ Total Equity

Earnings Before Interest, Taxes, Depreciation, and Amortization (EBITDA) Margin

This metric is used to assess a company's profitability by comparing its revenue with its core earnings. EBITDA *is earnings before interest, taxes, depreciation, and amortization.* Calculation:

EBITDA Margin = EBITDA ÷ Revenue

Days' Sales Outstanding (DSO)

DSO is the average number of days that a company takes to collect revenue after a sale has been made. A low DSO means that it takes the company fewer days to collect its accounts receivable. A high DSO means that a company is selling its products on credit and taking longer to collect payments. Calculation:

$$DSO = \text{Accounts Receivable} \div \text{Total Credit Sales}$$
$$\text{for a Period} \times \text{Number of Days in the Period}$$

THE VALUE OF METRICS IN SELLING TO THE C-SUITE

The key to using the metrics just described in the sales process is to understand the importance and relevance of your products or services to the financial levers that lead to your prospect's strategic buying decisions.

For example, if you sell a product that has a significant impact on DSOs, it is critical that you:

* Understand the meaning of DSOs.

* Understand the calculation of DSOs.

* Articulate your value as it relates to lowering DSOs.

The C-Suite effect takes place when you are able to communicate your value as it positively affects your prospect's C-Suite metrics. For example, an uninformed sales professional might say, "Gee, Mr. Customer, we can lower those DSOs for you, no problem." A better approach would be, "In the past we have lowered our customers' DSOs by as much as 10 days. In fact, last week I was talking to ABC Company, and we helped it reduce DSOs by almost three weeks." Note that in the second statement, you are specific about the impact of your product and provide proof of your success at other customers' sites.

Let's try another example. An uninformed sales professional might say, "Our products can help you sell more." A better approach is, "We have increased our customers' revenue as much as 10 percent in the past, leading to higher earnings and an increase in net profit. When you talk to our customers, you will hear them talk about 5 to 10 percent increases in profit margins."

When you are initially identifying a prospect's issues, pains, or goals (what we call "pain discovery"), it is important that you direct your discussion toward the impact on metrics like net profit margin, earnings, and operating costs rather than toward revenue increases or cost reductions. The financial levers that C-Suite executives rely on are based on the metrics, not the total revenue increases or cost reductions. Remember that the pain defined has a direct impact on the metrics that the C-Suite is using to make a strategic buying decision. Your conversation may sound something like this: "I understand your issues with rising labor costs and their effect on your financial reports. However, our automated system can help you with labor cost reduction and put *more profit on your bottom line, reducing your operating costs and increasing your net profit.*" This statement better defines your value as it relates to your prospect's financial goals and levers. Your impact is not only labor cost reduction, but operating cost reduction and increases in net profit margin, leading to higher earnings potential.

The fact that you mention the effect on your prospect's strategic financial levers will set you apart from competitors who are still selling features, benefits, and ROI. With a new focus on impact on the C-Suite, you will be able to shift the paradigm from you as a sales professional to you as a consultative sales expert.

SUMMARY

In this chapter, we identified and defined the key C-Suite metrics that C-Suite executives use to determine the organization's strategic direction and make purchasing decisions. Be sure you understand what these metrics mean and how they relate to your product's value.

Your role in the C-Suite effect involves communicating the impact that your product or service has on the financial reports, metrics, or levers that your prospect tracks and the overall financial health and well-being of the company you are trying to sell to. Remember these key points:

- Learn to use and master the financial vocabulary.

- Study and understand the C-Suite metrics and their calculations.

- Know your product's value as it relates to the C-Suite metrics.

- Through conversation, gain an understanding of what the C-Suite metrics mean to your prospect.

Using this concept will change the way you currently sell. You do not need to be a financial expert to understand the concept of the C-Suite effect. You do, however, need to understand how the metrics are represented and how they are calculated.

Strategic buying decisions are made at the C-level every day. These decisions are driven by their effect on a corporation's financial health and goals. The company's financial reports reflect whether it is expanding or contracting. You need to know if the company is in a cash crunch or is cash rich, whether it is profitable or going under. It is crucial that you understand your impact as it relates to the strategic direction in which an organization is heading. The C-Suite effect will help you with this understanding.

Chapter 2 outlines how to build your value inventory. This is a critical step toward understanding your value as it relates to the C-Suite metrics. You will need the concepts laid out in Chapter 1 to complete the exercises in Chapter 2. If you are still unclear as to the definition and calculation of these C-Suite metrics, keep a copy of the definitions nearby as you complete the value inventory exercise.

CHAPTER 2

BUILDING YOUR
VALUE INVENTORY

In his *Little Red Book of Selling* (Bard Press, 2004), Jeffrey Gitomer wrote, "Why do people buy is a billion times more important than how do I sell." I often wonder why organizations spend millions of dollars on teaching their sales professionals how to sell, but very few spend a dime on helping them to understand why their customers buy. This question is where we begin the journey of creating our value inventory.

THE USES OF A VALUE INVENTORY

Building a high-quality value inventory takes time and effort, but the payback comes tenfold. It is crucial to engage people from both sales and other areas in this effort. We believe that anyone who interacts with your customers should participate in the process of building a value inventory, if possible. These people probably will have an opinion as to why your customers bought your products and services in the first place, as well as how they are using and deploying them. The exercise in this chapter is designed to collect data on your customers so that you can use them to better understand your market and its issues, and the value of your products and services as it relates to the problems that you solve for customers. Building your value inventory will serve as the foundation for correlating value to the C-Suite metrics discussed in Chapter 1.

CREATING A VALUE INVENTORY MATRIX

To begin the process of building your value inventory, create a matrix in a spreadsheet program like Microsoft Excel®, with the following headings: "Why Buy?," "Business Issue," "Desired Outcome," "Stakeholder," "Solution," "Value Metric," "Value Proposition," and "C-Suite Impact" (see Figure 2-1).

FIGURE 2-1

Why Buy?	Business Issue	Desired Outcome	Stakeholder	Solution	Value Metric	Value Proposition	C-Suite Impact

The completion of this matrix is the foundation for building and deploying sales tools for each phase of your sales process. It is critical to your success to gather a diverse group of customer-facing personnel, such as:

- *Sales professionals.* This exercise will provide valuable insight into why your customers buy from you, and specifically what value your products and services provide to your customers. In addition, upon completion of this exercise, you and your team's confidence level as it relates to your organization's ability to deliver high-value solutions will typically increase.

- *Marketing staff.* Creating a value inventory is a natural extension of marketing's primary job: creating interest in your products and services. The problem has been and continues to be that Marketing and Sales seem to be on different planes. According to a study by the American Marketing Association, more than 80 percent of the materials that Marketing produces are never used in the sales process. By participating in this exercise together, marketing and sales professionals will become closer. They will begin to see each other's point of view and better understand exactly what you sell, the problems that you solve, and more precisely who your target (stakeholder) market really is.

- *Direct support personnel.* This is an opportunity for the members of your support staff to discuss the issues they are dealing with when they talk to your customers. It is not uncommon for a frustrated customer to say, "I bought this system to do x, y, and z. Why doesn't it do what I was sold?" Support staff can provide valuable insight into the challenges *after the sale.* This can provide important lessons to Sales and Marketing, and to your management team.

- *Consulting professionals.* Your consultants are on the front lines, taking the accolades when things go well and hits for the potential missteps in the sales process. By being part of this exercise, your consulting team will learn the sales team's point of view and management's expectations as to what the products should be doing and how they should be performing. Conversely, the rest of the team will get insight into the reality of implementing your solutions. Consultants are very helpful in the process; bringing them into it provides you with an opportunity to educate them on the potential for cross-selling and upselling.

- *Sales and marketing management.* Your leaders need to be present, but they cannot dominate the discussion. Give them their say in the process, but allow/enable the rest of the participants to have the opportunity to complete the matrix. Management can provide good insight into its intention when a product or service is created. However, when it comes to the practical use of this creation, managers tend to want to take over the conversation. They too can learn a lot from Sales, Support, and Consulting as well as how Marketing is promoting the products and services.

The diversity of the participants in this exercise is important. Differing views of the same issue will add a great deal of insight into why your customers do what they do. Let's begin with the first column of our matrix.

Why Buy?

The first step in building your value inventory is to put yourself in your customer's shoes. (Pick the customer stakeholder whom you deal with the most.) Ask yourself why "you" bought in the first place. When you try to think like your customer, you are able to provide a unique perspective based on your position within your organization. This is the primary reason that you want customer-facing personnel in this exercise: to gather the point of view of as many stakeholders as possible. (More on how important this is later.) Each person in this workshop should select a stakeholder whom he communicates with regularly and "put himself in that person's shoes." The premise behind this concept is to be emotional about your issues, pains, and goals. Begin each sentence with "We" (or "I") and answer the following question: *Why buy products and services like yours?* Typical responses might be:

- "We need to lower our labor costs."

- "We need to reduce our overhead costs."

- "We need to reduce shrinkage."

- "We need to stop discounting so much."

- "We need to stop coming in second so often."

- "We need to sell more and expand our market share."

Keep it emotional in the first column ("Why Buy?"). Don't overthink the process. Keep it simple, and use 10 words or fewer to describe why you (the prospect) would buy products and services like the ones you sell.

WHAT ABOUT HAVING CUSTOMERS PARTICIPATE
WHEN YOU ARE BUILDING YOUR VALUE INVENTORY?

Our experience has been that this can be somewhat revealing with regard to product weaknesses and potential service issues. The value inventory workshop is intended, first, to capture your value from your customer's point of view, and second, to focus your team on that value. Exposing a limitation in your products or services could be harmful to your relationship with the customer who is sitting in on the meeting. However, if your relationship with this customer is one of trust and understanding, it is a great idea to have her participate.

As you begin to complete the value inventory, be aware of duplication in the why-buy statements. Try to limit the discussion to the top 25 or so answers. Be sure to get answers from everyone involved in the process because you want as much diversity as you can possibly get.

Figure 2-2 is an example of the first column of a value inventory based on one of our customers.

Notice the simplicity of the why-buy statements. They are short, to the point, and emotional in nature. Remember to always begin your sentence with "WE" or "I." This will keep you pointed in the right direction and force you to use emotion when entering the answer.

FIGURE 2-2

Why Buy?	Business Issue	Desired Outcome	Stakeholder	Solution	Value Metric	Value Proposition	C-Suite Impact
We need to lower our DSOs							
We need to reduce our labor costs							
We need to reduce discounting							
We need to reduce customer attrition							

Business Issue

The next column is "Business Issue." The business issue begins to narrow down the why-buy response to something more measurable. Read the why-buy sentence aloud and tack on this phrase: "for what reason?" For example, using the value matrix from our customer in Figure 2-2, "We need to reduce our labor costs, for what reason?" A typical response might be, "Because our burden, overhead, and/or inflation have caused our labor costs to continue to rise." Or perhaps, "Because our labor costs are taking up too much of our total budget."

The key to an acceptable business-issue statement is the ability to articulate the answer to "Why Buy?" with a measurable pain. In other words, can you identify the pain and establish a cost for it based on the business-issue statement? Figure 2-3 gives the business-issue answers from our customer's value inventory.

Once again, notice the simplicity in the answers. Each sentence begins with "because" and includes a reason and something that can be measured. (The actual measurement in numbers or percentages will come later.) Remember, the most important part of your answer to the business issue is a measurable response. See Table 2-1.

FIGURE 2-3

Why Buy?	Business Issue	Desired Outcome	Stakeholder	Solution	Value Metric	Value Proposition	C-Suite Impact
We need to lower our DSOs	because we are losing interest income						
We need to reduce our labor costs	because our labor costs continue to rise						
We need to reduce discounting	because we are losing revenue						
We need to reduce customer attrition	because we are losing revenue and our cost to acquire new customers is rising						

TABLE 2-1

Why-Buy Statement	Unit of Measure (Cost Metric)
Need to lower DSOs	Loss of interest income
Need to reduce labor costs	Constant increase in labor costs
Need to reduce discounting	Loss of revenue
Need to reduce customer attrition	Loss of revenue

Desired Outcome

The "Desired Outcome" column is our last attempt to capture the unit of measure (cost metric) when identifying pain. Remember, when you are done, you want to be able to take this document and create a financial-based pain-discovery questionnaire, total cost of ownership (TCO) program, value estimation model, and/or other financial-based sales tools. Therefore, it is crucial that you get this column correct now. When entering the data for desired outcome, you will want to read the why-buy and business-issue statements out loud in the form of a sentence. For example, "We need to reduce our labor costs because they are taking up too much of our total budget." Next add the words, "Therefore I want to achieve what?" The key to a successful desired-outcome statement is your ability to state the issues in terms of quantity of pain at this moment, and what you want as a desired result in the future.

For example, "We need to reduce our labor costs because they are taking up too much of our total budget"; therefore, "We want to reduce the percentage of labor costs in our operating budget." This may be a bit wordy; however, it achieves the goal of being able to identify a problem, measure the current impact of that problem, and then return at a time in the future and repeat the effort. The reason for this is that if you identify pain and measure the current cost, it establishes a baseline for measuring the value you have delivered in the future (*basically an ROI calculation*). See the value inventory in Figure 2-4, which includes the "Desired Outcome" column completed, and the baseline measurements in Table 2-2.

FIGURE 2-4

Why Buy?	Business Issue	Desired Outcome	Stakeholder	Solution	Value Metric	Value Proposition	C-Suite Impact
We need to lower our DSOs	because we are losing interest income	therefore we want to increase our annual interest income					
We need to reduce our labor costs	because our labor costs continue to rise	therefore we want to reduce our labor costs					
We need to reduce discounting	because we are losing revenue	therefore we want to reduce our average discount rate					
We need to reduce customer attrition	because we are losing revenue and our cost to acquire new customers is rising	therefore we want to recapture lost revenue and lower our cost of new customer acquisition					

TABLE 2-2

Why-Buy Statement	Unit of Measure (Cost Metric)	Baseline Measurement
Need to lower DSOs	Loss of interest income	Current annual interest lost because of extended DSOs
Need to reduce labor costs	Constant increase in labor costs	Current labor cost—payroll as a percentage of total revenue, revenue per employee
Need to reduce discounting	Loss of revenue	Annual revenue lost because of discounting
Need to reduce customer attrition	Loss of revenue	Annual revenue lost because of customer attrition

Notice that the baseline measurement for reducing labor cost is "current labor cost." However, we listed some additional metrics that we believe are important to know about. When you want to affect the labor cost of an organization, you need to look beyond the cost factor. Metrics like payroll as a percentage of revenue or revenue per employee are as important as the actual cost of labor. Labor cost reductions or labor cost avoidances will affect the metrics in positive ways. A small reduction in labor cost can have a big impact on the C-Suite metrics. Senior executives will respond positively to any cuts in labor costs, now or down the road.

Stakeholder

The stakeholder is a key component of the usefulness of this exercise. You need to know who in the strategic decision-making process is affected most by your products and services. At the beginning of this exercise, we told you to "put yourself in your customer's shoes." Now the time has come to tell us who you are. The stakeholder process is designed to tie problems to people. This step will enable you to understand who within an organization has the power to buy from you and who can make it difficult for you to sell.

In addition to identifying the stakeholder, we suggest that you create a list of stakeholders who will share the pain based on the problem defined. This string of stakeholders identifies your allies and your enemies in your prospect's organization, the people whom each line item in your value inventory affects most. Who has the most to gain or lose by making a decision to buy from you? For example, if the stakeholder is the CFO, then the decision to buy from you may affect the chief technology officer (CTO), the human resources (HR) director, and other executives within an organization. The additional executives may have the ability to stop a purchase in its tracks, and they probably have their own set of metrics that they track.

This exercise forces you to understand the concept of "selling broad and deep" within a prospect's organization. Figure 2-5 displays a completed "Stakeholder" column.

FIGURE 2-5

Why Buy?	Business Issue	Desired Outcome	Stakeholder	Solution	Value Metric	Value Proposition	C-Suite Impact
We need to lower our DSOs	because we are losing interest income	therefore we want to increase our annual interest income	CFO, CEO				
We need to reduce our labor costs	because our labor costs continue to rise	therefore we want to reduce our labor costs	VP HR, GM, CFO				
We need to reduce discounting	because we are losing revenue	therefore we want to reduce our average discount rate	VP Sales, CFO, CEO				
We need to reduce customer attrition	because we are losing revenue and our cost to acquire new customers is rising	therefore we want to recapture lost revenue and lower our cost of new customer acquisition	VP Customer Service, VP Sales				

Problems are tied to people. You need to know who is affected most by the purchase of your products and services.

Solution

Notice that throughout this process, you haven't been asked about your product or service. This is by design. The objective of creating a value inventory is to capture information based on your customer list and prospects, not your features and benefits. By focusing on the prospect's issues, pains, and goals, and not on the solutions, you are forcing more credibility into your analysis and more objectivity into your process. As you work your way through this exercise, think about the value you can deliver as you discuss the issues that your customers and prospects are facing.

For this column, focus on a solution, not necessarily a single feature or benefit. Solutions may include many features, benefits, modules, or perhaps products and services that you sell, either on their own or in combination. A key point regarding solutions is that they must be measurable. Your solution must reduce a cost, help avoid a cost (like the need to hire additional personnel), and/or increase revenue. (More on this in a moment.)

(*Note:* Because of the complex nature of the solutions you will come up with and the fact that they are unique to your company's products or services, we will simply insert placeholders into the "Solution" column of our sample value inventory to avoid confusion. When you are filling out the matrix for one of your own customers, of course, you will go through the full range of possible solutions in order to determine the best one for any given situation.)

Once you have identified and documented your solution (keep it short), you are going to have to provide the solution's value metric and the value proposition delivered. (See Figure 2-6.)

Value Metric

The value metric identifies the solution's value as it relates to solving the issue, pain, or goal. In this column, you will enter one or more of the following: "Reduce cost," "Avoid cost," and/or "Increase revenue."

FIGURE 2-6

Why Buy?	Business Issue	Desired Outcome	Stakeholder	Solution	Value Metric	Value Proposition	C-Suite Impact
We need to lower our DSOs	because we are losing interest income	therefore we want to increase our annual interest income	CFO, CEO	Solution A			
We need to reduce our labor costs	because our labor costs continue to rise	therefore we want to reduce our labor costs	VP HR, GM, CFO	Solution B			
We need to reduce discounting	because we are losing revenue	therefore we want to reduce our average discount rate	VP Sales, CFO, CEO	Solution C			
We need to reduce customer attrition	because we are losing revenue and our cost to acquire new customers is rising	therefore we want to recapture lost revenue and lower our cost of new customer acquisition	VP Customer Service, VP Sales	Solution D			

A *cost reduction* reduces an existing cost that the customer is currently incurring as part of his daily business activity. Examples of cost reductions include:

- Labor costs
- Material costs
- Fines or penalties
- Supplies
- Shipping or transport costs
- Overhead or operating costs
- Depreciation
- Tax liability
- Shrinkage

A *cost avoidance* provides customers with an opportunity to avoid incurring an additional cost to what they are currently paying. Examples of cost avoidances include:

* Avoid hiring additional personnel.

* Avoid purchasing additional materials.

* Avoid physically shipping documents, parts, equipment, and so on.

* Avoid paying fines or penalties.

Finally, *revenue increases* are additions to the customer's total revenue. Examples include:

* Increase in average sale amount

* Increase in number of products sold per customer

* Increase in margin

* Reduction in discounting, leading to additional revenue

* Reduction in attrition, increasing what was lost revenue in the first place

* Eliminating discounts, thus adding to revenue

> **KEY POINT**
> The goal of this exercise is to identify pain, tie the pain to a stakeholder, and establish a solution that is measurable.

Ultimately, this document becomes your foundation for building financial-based sales tools that are capable of measuring cost reductions, revenue increases, or cost avoidances. The key to filling in the "Value Metric" column is to realize that your prospect's problems can be measured and your solution can be valued. At this point, stick to these three options—reduce a cost, avoid a cost, or increase revenue—and stay away from "profit" for now. (We will deal with it later.)

One last point to remember is that to improve your margin, you must either reduce a cost or increase your revenue. Sometimes you are able to do both and see an even larger increase in margin. See our value inventory in Figure 2-7.

FIGURE 2-7

Why Buy?	Business Issue	Desired Outcome	Stakeholder	Solution	Value Metric	Value Proposition	C-Suite Impact
We need to lower our DSOs	because we are losing interest income	therefore we want to increase our annual interest income	CFO, CEO	Solution A	Increase revenue		
We need to reduce our labor costs	because our labor costs continue to rise	therefore we want to reduce our labor costs	VP HR, GM, CFO	Solution B	Reduce cost		
We need to reduce discounting	because we are losing revenue	therefore we want to reduce our average discount rate	VP Sales, CFO, CEO	Solution C	Increase revenue		
We need to reduce customer attrition	because we are losing revenue and our cost to acquire new customers is rising	therefore we want to recapture lost revenue and lower our cost of new customer acquisition	VP Customer Service, VP Sales	Solution D	Increase revenue, reduce cost		

Value Proposition

The next step requires you to define what the metric you entered into the value inventory is specifically referring to. In other words, if you are reducing a cost, what cost are you reducing? If you are increasing revenue, what type of revenue is being increased? (See the previous lists of sample reductions and increases.) Situations arise where your value extends to both increases in revenue and reductions in cost. It is okay to document that, too. For example, in the bottom row of the matrix in Figure 2-8, customer attrition can drive an increase in revenue by recapturing lost customers and reducing the cost to acquire new customers.

The completed matrix in Figure 2-8 will help you to better understand what is required in developing a solid value inventory. Keep in mind that one of the assets of a value inventory is the ability to identify pain and quantify that pain. In addition, the value inventory provides you with the opportunity to identify a solution to the pain. This is important to understand because a value matrix is typically not developed by product; it is developed by solution. Look at your market and say to yourself, What problems do we solve? If you can stay focused on solutions and not products, you will be better served by the results.

FIGURE 2-8

Why Buy?	Business Issue	Desired Outcome	Stakeholder	Solution	Value Metric	Value Proposition	C-Suite Impact
We need to lower our DSOs	because we are losing interest income	therefore we want to increase our annual interest income	CFO, CEO	Solution A	Increase revenue	Intrest income	
We need to reduce our labor costs	because our labor costs continue to rise	therefore we want to reduce our labor costs	VP HR, GM, CFO	Solution B	Reduce cost	Human capital	
We need to reduce discounting	because we are losing revenue	therefore we want to reduce our average discount rate	VP Sales, CFO, CEO	Solution C	Increase revenue	Capture lost revenue from discounting	
We need to reduce customer attrition	because we are losing revenue and our cost to acquire new customers is rising	therefore we want to recapture lost revenue and lower our cost of new customer acquisition	VP Customer Service, VP Sales	Solution D	Increase revenue, reduce cost	Recapture lost revenue, reduce cost per customer to acquire	

C-SUITE IMPACT

Now that you have completed your value inventory, we suggest that you share the results with your company's CFO (chief financial officer), vice president of finance, controller, or financial advisor. Ask her if she can help you identify the C-Suite metrics that are affected by the value ("Value Metric" column) that you have established that you can deliver ("Solution" column). Have your financial advisor explain to you why each metric is affected and in what way. In other words, if you can help a prospect reduce his labor cost, then be sure you understand the impact of your solution on operating cost reductions, net profit increases, or perhaps earnings increases. Work through each line with the financial person and discuss the C-Suite impact of your solution.

Be sure to document these discussions in the last column, called "C-Suite Impact." Later we will discuss the actual impact calculations and how to use this information to position your product or service when talking to your prospect's C-level executives. Figure 2-9 shows the value inventory completely filled out, including the C-suite impact.

FIGURE 2-9

Why Buy?	Business Issue	Desired Outcome	Stakeholder	Solution	Value Metric	Value Proposition	C-Suite Impact
We need to lower our DSOs	because we are losing interest income	therefore we want to increase our annual interest income	CFO, CEO	Solution A	Increase revenue	Intrest income	Earnings, operating costs net profit
We need to reduce our labor costs	because our labor costs continue to rise	therefore we want to reduce our labor costs	VP HR, GM, CFO	Solution B	Reduce cost	Human capital	Operating costs, net profit
We need to reduce discounting	because we are losing revenue	therefore we want to reduce our average discount rate	VP Sales, CFO, CEO	Solution C	Increase revenue	Capture lost revenue from discounting	Net profit, earnings
We need to reduce customer attrition	because we are losing revenue and our cost to acquire new customers is rising	therefore we want to recapture lost revenue and lower our cost of new customer acquisition	VP Customer Service, VP Sales	Solution D	Increase revenue, reduce cost	Recapture lost revenue, reduce cost per customer to acquire	Net profit, earnings, operating costs

KEY POINT

It is not necessary to learn and memorize the meaning of and calculations for all the C-Suite metrics. It is, however, necessary to learn the metrics that apply to your value inventory. Keep these definitions close as you work through the steps in this book.

SUMMARY

Organizations spend millions of dollars on training sales professionals how to sell and very little or nothing on understanding why their customers buy from them. How can you expect to be successful at selling when you don't understand why people buy from you?

Creating your value inventory is a big step toward selling to C-Suite executives. Properly filled out, it will help you to:

* Create financial-based sales tools.

* Understand industry issues and how your value relates to them.

* Tie people to problems—enhance your focus on stakeholders.

- Drive confidence within the sales force that your products and services will solve real issues and pains.

- Bring your team members together on the same page.

- Provide new hires with a training tool.

When building your value inventory, be sure to invite your top sales professionals, marketing personnel, direct support team, and consulting group—and don't forget your sales and marketing management. Customer-facing personnel will enrich your effort to get a diversity of opinions as to why people buy your products and services.

Your value inventory should always begin with emotion. "Why buy?" is an emotional question. Once you have exhausted the emotional responses, move on to more logical and measurable responses, such as the business issue and desired outcome. Finally, focus on the stakeholder. Stakeholders are a key component of the sales process. You will need to identify those people within your prospect's organization who have the most to gain and the most to lose. Too often, we get comfortable with one or two stakeholders and never move beyond this and look for those people who do not want our solution. Remember, you need to sell broad and deep within an organization.

This chapter provided several examples of cost reductions, cost avoidances, and revenue increases. The most confusing area is the difference between cost reductions and cost avoidances. Measuring cost avoidances is not always that simple. Focus on your ability to help your prospect "avoid" having to invest money to fix a problem, as opposed to reducing the amount of money that is already being spent.

Remember, your value inventory will ultimately become your foundation for building financial-based sales tools.

The C-Suite effect is achieved when you are able to identify your value and relate it to the C-Suite metrics defined in the first chapter. Now that you have completed this chapter, you will have a better understanding of your value proposition and how it affects those financial metrics. Keep in mind that C-level executives will use these financial levers to make strategic buying decisions. Those metrics include net and gross profit margin, return on assets (ROA), return on equity (ROE), earnings, debt-to-equity ratio, and more. It is crucial that when you are developing your value inventory, you take the additional step of including the C-Suite impact in your document. We strongly suggest that you discuss your value and the C-Suite metrics with your own financial advisors or CFO.

In addition, your value inventory will help you bridge the gap between your sales process, methodology, and training. The value inventory can be used for:

- New hire training
- Precall planning
- Elevator speech development
- Updating your web site and marketing literature
- Identifying areas on which to focus marketing campaigns
- Identifying and targeting stakeholders more effectively
- Bonding exercises with sales and marketing
- Building confidence within your team regarding your value proposition

Once you have completed your value inventory and the foundation is established, you are able to move on to the next step—creating the questions that will drive your prospect back to you for the value that you are able to deliver.

In Chapter 3, we take the value inventory that you have created and develop the pain-discovery questions that will bring your prospect to you for a solution. These questions will:

- Help establish the prospect's pain.
- Capture the current cost of pain.
- Extrapolate pain over time.
- Prove that the status quo is not free.

IDENTIFYING YOUR PROSPECT'S THRESHOLD FOR PAIN

In this chapter, you will learn how to turn your value inventory into a series of quantitatively based discovery questions that will help you accomplish three primary objectives:

1. You will be better able to identify pain, capture it, and calculate its current cost.

2. You will learn how to prove to your prospect that maintaining the status quo is not free.

3. You will be transformed from a "sales professional" to a "consultative sales expert."

These three objectives cover a great deal of material. Be sure you are prepared by completing your value inventory.

USING YOUR VALUE INVENTORY TO CREATE DISCOVERY QUESTIONS

We assume that you already know your product's features and benefits and have the ability to identify a qualified prospect. Let's begin with the results of your value inventory (see Figure 3-1).

FIGURE 3-1

Why Buy?	Business Issue	Desired Outcome	Stakeholder	Solution	Value Metric	Value Proposition	C-Suite Impact
We need to lower our DSOs	because we are losing interest income	therefore we want to increase our annual interest income	CFO, CEO	Solution A	Increase revenue	Intrest income	Earnings, operating costs net profit
We need to reduce our labor costs	because our labor costs continue to rise	therefore we want to reduce our labor costs	VP HR, GM, CFO	Solution B	Reduce cost	Human capital	Operating costs, net profit
We need to reduce discounting	because we are losing revenue	therefore we want to reduce our average discount rate	VP Sales, CFO, CEO	Solution C	Increase revenue	Capture lost revenue from discounting	Net profit, earnings
We need to reduce customer attrition	because we are losing revenue and our cost to acquire new customers is rising	therefore we want to recapture lost revenue and lower our cost of new customer acquisition	VP Customer Service, VP Sales	Solution D	Increase revenue, reduce cost	Recapture lost revenue, reduce cost per customer to acquire	Net profit, earnings, operating costs

If you were successful in creating your value inventory, you're ready to move on to the next steps. If not, you may have some challenges in completing the next set of exercises. Go back and reread Chapter 2. Make sure that you fully understand how to create your value inventory, because this step is critical to building your C-Suite business case.

There is an old adage, don't ask the question unless you know the answer. This rings true in many (but not all) sales situations. Your success lies in your ability to identify pain through a series of questions, and to reach an agreement with your prospects as to their current cost and their *threshold for pain* (the tipping point at which a prospect is going to buy something).

> **KEY POINT**
>
> Each line of your value inventory tells a story of pain that your prospects may be facing. This pain must be identified, agreed upon, and measured or calculated. Once you and a prospect agree on the pain and the cost of the pain, you are able to extrapolate that cost over time and discuss the threshold for pain and the cost of the status quo. The point you ultimately want to make to the prospect is, "Keeping the status quo and delaying a decision is not *free!*"

The process of converting your value inventory into a series of questions will help you identify issues, pains, and goals; capture current costs; and extrapolate those costs over a period of three to seven years. This transition of your value inventory to a discovery questionnaire is crucial to your success in selling to C-level executives. We will review the steps in developing a basic pain-discovery questionnaire that you can ultimately use throughout your sales process.

Use a spreadsheet program to enter your questions and answers. Throughout the book, we will provide some additional information on what your screens should look like. Later you will need to access the data that you collected from your questions and use them in several dashboard calculations and ultimately in building your C-Suite business case.

CREATING YOUR PAIN-DISCOVERY QUESTIONS

The questions that you create will establish the foundation for the pain-discovery or bonding phase of your sales process. At this point, let's assume that you have qualified your prospect. Does your prospect meet your marketing criteria? Does your prospect have a means to purchase your product or service? Does your prospect have a motive to purchase your product or service? Be sure to establish right away a basis for what you would call a "qualified" prospect.

The questions that you create are going to be used to identify pain and capture current cost. This is a crucial step in your sales process (and sales methodology) because it will eventually become the basis for connecting your value to your prospect's financial reports, i.e., the C-Suite effect. The questions stem from each line of the value inventory. When you created your value inventory, we asked you to put yourself in your prospect's shoes, identify issues that you (that prospect) are facing, and then come up with your solution. Armed with this information, you now have all the possible reasons that someone would buy from you. This is a very powerful document. Think about it: You have in your hands every answer to the question, why buy my product? However, what you are missing are the questions that drive your prospect back to you to buy your value proposition.

Keep in mind that your value inventory (Figure 3-2) reveals not only the reasons to buy, but also the stakeholders whom you should be talking to—a list of who has the most to gain and lose by purchasing or implementing your products or services—and finally your solution to the issue, pain, or goal that you identified.

FIGURE 3-2

Why Buy	Business Issue	Desired Outcome	Stakeholder	Solution	Value Metric	Value Proposition	C-Suite Impact
We need to lower our DSOs	because we are losing interest income	therefore we want to increase our annual income	CFO, CEO	Solution A	Increase revenue	Increase income	Earnings, operating cost, net profit
We need to reduce our labor costs	because our labor costs continue to rise	therefore we want to reduce our labor costs	VP HR, GM, CFO	Solution B	Reduce cost	Human capital	Operating costs, new profit
We need to reduce discounting	because we are losing revenue	therefore we want to reduce our average discount rate	VP Sales, CFO, CEO	Solution C	Increase revenue	Capture cost revenue from discounting	Net profit, earnings
We need to reduce customer attrition	because we are losing revenue and our csots to acquire new cusomters is rising	therefore we want to recapture lost revenue and lower our costs of new customer acquisition	VP Customer Service, VP Sales	Solution D	Increase revenue, reduce cost	Recapture lost revenue, reduce cost per customer to acquire	Net profit, earnings, operating costs

The first step in creating pain-discovery questions is to establish the unit of measure and the pain point. Table 3-1 has headings for desired outcome, unit of measure, pain point defined, and the questions that will capture the information we need in order to establish the status quo.

TABLE 3-1

Desired Outcome	Unit of Measure	Pain Point	Current Cost Questions
Reduce discounting	Average annual discount rate	Lost revenue from discounting	1. Annual revenue 2. Average annual discount

As an example, we selected the third line of the value inventory. In this line, the prospect's issue is clearly excessive discounting. The primary unit of measure is the average annual discount rate. In other words, the whole reason this problem exists is that the average annual discount rate is too high. The prospect's sales force is giving away too much of its sales opportunities in discounts. So the pain point is the amount of revenue lost as a result of having too high a discount rate. To establish the status quo, you need to ask yourself, "How do I get to the amount of revenue that is lost each year as a result of excessive discounting?" Obviously this is the pain point from Table 3-1. It is also the unit of measure that we are going to use to calculate the pain: lost revenue.

Once you have established the unit of measure and the pain point, your questions should drive the prospect back to both the pain itself and the current cost. For example, you know from the completed value inventory that certain things about your customer are true. First, discounting is an issue. Second, you can resolve this issue (solution and metric)—and therefore you know that your value proposition is to help the prospect reduce discounting.

So you want to create questions that will let you better understand a prospect's pain from excessive discounting. However, first you want the prospect to "buy in" to the pain and the cost of that pain. Ask two simple questions: "What is your annual revenue?" and "What is your average discount?" Once you get the answers to these two questions, you are able to calculate the prospect's annual loss from discounting. Annual revenue loss is the pain that drives the action. The action is purchasing from you to help reduce the amount of revenue that is being lost as a result of the sales force's excessive discounting.

> **KEY POINT**
>
> When creating tools to be used to sell to the C-Suite, it is crucial to understand your need to capture, share, and get buy-in on information that the prospect "doesn't already know." In this case, it could be the amount of revenue lost each year to discounting. Ask the question, confirm the answer, calculate, and extrapolate the cost of the status quo to the prospect.

Here is the simple calculation that you can use to illustrate your prospect's annual loss from discounting:

Annual revenue: $50,000,000

Average annual discount: 12%

Calculated cost of annual discount: $6,818,182

This exercise must be performed for each of the value propositions in your value inventory. Once you have developed the value calculations, you can create pain-discovery questions like, "Are you losing revenue from excessive discounting?" or "Are your financials (earnings or net profit) affected by the revenue lost from discounting?" These discovery questions will set up the groundwork for establishing the pain, capturing current cost, and driving your prospect back to you for a solution.

Table 3-2 gives another example from our sample value inventory.

TABLE 3-2

Desired Outcome	Unit of Measure	Pain Point	Current Cost Questions
Reduce customer attrition	Attrition rate	Lost revenue from lost customers	1. Number of customers 2. Annual attrition rate 3. Annual revenue from customer base

1. Number of customers

2. Annual attrition rate

3. Annual revenue from customer base

In this example, the problem is a loss of revenue as a result of customer attrition, a common problem for many businesses. Most organizations don't really track their losses from attrition or fully understand the impact of a lost customer. There are four key points that you need to know in order to calculate the annual revenue lost from customer attrition:

1. Number of customers generating revenue

2. Annual attrition rate for the customer base

3. Revenue per lost customer

4. Annual revenue that the existing customers generate

With these four points, you are able to calculate:

* Number of customers lost per year

* Annual revenue lost per year

* The effect that attrition can have on the prospect's financial statements

Here is the mathematics used to calculate the annual revenue lost each year from customer attrition:

Number of customers: 1,750

Annual revenue from customers: $11,350,000

Annual attrition rate: 8%

With 1,750 customers generating $11,350,000 and an annual attrition rate of 8 percent, you are able to calculate the annual revenue loss to be $908,000.

$$\$11,350,000 \div 1,750 = \$6,486 \text{ (value of each lost customer)}$$

$$1,750 \times 8\% = 140 \text{ (number of lost customers)}$$

$$140 \times \$6,486 = \$908,000 \text{ (annual revenue loss from customer attrition)}$$

Thinking in terms of the C-Suite effect, once you have calculated the annual revenue loss from customer attrition, you are able to discuss the impact on not only the company's annual revenue, but also other C-Suite metrics such as earnings; revenue per employee; profit; operating costs as a percentage of revenue; and, of course, shareholder value. Remember, it is not just about the ROI anymore. It is about the C-Suite effect.

Finally, once you have worked through your value inventory and identified the desired outcomes, units of measure, and pain points, be sure to create the pain-discovery questions that drive your prospect back to you to solve the issue. For example, you may ask the question, "Is customer attrition cutting into your profit margins?" or perhaps, "Is customer attrition affecting shareholder value?" These pain-discovery questions will help drive prospects back to your solution based on the value that you can deliver and the effect on the C-Suite metrics and strategic buying decision process. Pain-discovery questions are the foundation for precall planning and the bonding and rapport phase of your sales process: identifying pain, capturing current cost, and discussing your solution that delivers value to your prospect.

Figure 3-3 is an example of how you can lay out the questions.

FIGURE 3-3

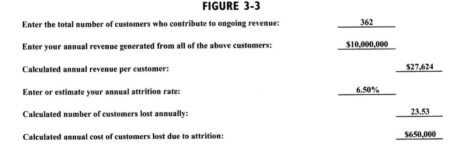

Enter the total number of customers who contribute to ongoing revenue:	362
Enter your annual revenue generated from all of the above customers:	$10,000,000
Calculated annual revenue per customer:	$27,624
Enter or estimate your annual attrition rate:	6.50%
Calculated number of customers lost annually:	23.53
Calculated annual cost of customers lost due to attrition:	$650,000

In this example you see how to get to the pain of losing $650,000 by asking just three questions—"How many customers do you have?" "What is your annual revenue?" and "Approximately what is your annual attrition rate?" Then do the math to display the cost of losing 6.5 percent of your customer base.

DETERMINING THE PROSPECT'S THRESHOLD FOR PAIN

The threshold for pain is the point at which a prospect has reached her limit in terms of the amount of pain she can handle. As you can see from Figure 3-4, the pain level is on the vertical axis and time is on the horizontal axis. The line moving from left to right at an angle is the pain line. (Obviously pain will not rise at a perfect 45-degree angle; however, for the purpose of this example, we will display it moving up in that manner.) The point we are trying to make is that as time continues to pass and the pain continues to increase, there comes a point when the person who is feeling the pain must make a decision to relieve herself of the pain. The point at which that occurs is the threshold for pain or tipping point.

The data you have collected through the questions that you created will help establish the current costs. The key to determining the threshold for pain is to be able to calculate an ongoing cost of maintaining the status quo. One certainty that we have all experienced in sales is that we lose to the status quo more often than we do to a competitor. Why is that? Simply, the prospect has not yet reached the threshold for pain. This means that we try to close too soon, and the prospect is not ready to be closed. He has not come to the conclusion that he cannot "take the pain" any longer. It is your responsibility as a consultative sales professional to help him to:

- Identify and agree on the pain defined.

- Capture and calculate the current cost of the status quo.

- Calculate the future cost of the status quo.

FIGURE 3-4

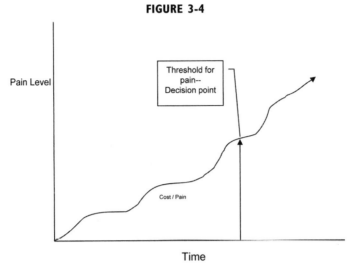

You need to first get buy-in from your prospect that the pain exists. After performing the discovery questionnaire, ask your prospect, "Do we agree that this is an issue that you are facing, and is the current cost of the issue correct?" Once you get validation, your next set of questions must be ones that help you capture, calculate, and extrapolate the future cost of the status quo.

In our previous example, we discussed the annual loss of revenue occurring as a result of customer attrition. Here are the calculations that we used:

With 1,750 customers generating $11,350,000 and an annual attrition rate of 8 percent, you are able to calculate the annual revenue loss as $908,000.

$$\$11,350,000 \div 1,750 = \$6,486 \text{ (value of each lost customer)}$$

$$1,750 \times 8\% = 140 \text{ (lost customers)}$$

$$140 \times \$6,486 = \$908,000 \text{ (annual loss from customer attrition)}$$

The components of customer attrition are the number of customers, the annual revenue that they are generating, and the attrition rate. To calculate the cost of the status quo in the future, you will want to discuss with your prospect the *expected customer growth and future revenue growth.* Keep in mind that any change in either customer growth or revenue growth will increase the loss of revenue through customer attrition (even when the attrition rate remains the same). For example:

Current annual revenue: $11,350,000

Current number of customers: 1,750

Current attrition rate: 8 percent

Ask the question, "What is your revenue growth forecast for next year and the year after?" or "What are your revenue goals for next year and the year after?" If your prospect says something like, "We estimate a 10 percent increase this year and 14 percent the year after," then you have a baseline for calculating the future cost of attrition. See Table 3-3 for how to perform the calculations for future revenue loss and the cost of the status quo.

TABLE 3-3

	Current	Year 2	Year 3
Revenue	$11,350,000	$12,485,000	$14,232,900
Customers	1,750	1,925	2,195
Attrition	140	154	176
Lost revenue	$908,000	$998,844	$1,141,536
Total loss		$1,906,844	$3,048,380

This simple table highlights two major points. First, if your prospect's attrition rate remains the same and the company continues to grow, the losses will increase. Second, if your prospect doesn't fix the problem of customer attrition by reducing the attrition rate or percentage, she stands to lose more than $3 million in a three-year period. Graphically, it will look like Figure 3-5.

FIGURE 3-5

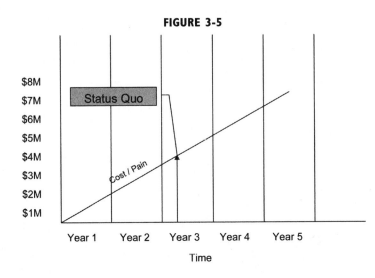

As a professional sales consultant, you will now want to have the discussion on the threshold for pain. When you show the issue graphically, you can simply ask, "Where on the pain line are you going to make a decision to fix your attrition problem?" or, "How much do you need to lose before you do something about the losses from attrition?" Of course, this assumes that you have a solution that will help this prospect reduce his customer attrition problem.

Helping your prospects calculate the cost of the status quo and discussing their threshold for pain will ensure that you are chasing an opportunity that has a higher probability of closing because you will be looked upon as a trusted advisor.

These fundamental principles hold true in most industries. Whether you sell software or backhoes, the point remains the same: When a prospect hits her threshold for pain, she will find a way to resolve the problem. It is important that you are armed with the tools to help her realize the pain and calculate the cost of that pain, and that you provide the visual to determine the prospect's threshold for pain.

ESTIMATING YOUR VALUE TO THE PROSPECT

Once you have created your questions to identify pain, capture and calculate cost, and determine the prospect's threshold for pain, you will want to establish your potential value. This is not as simple as saying, "I believe we can cut your attrition by 25 percent over the next three years. How does that sound to you?"

There are many factors involved in determining how to handle what you do next. Begin with what you have been able to do with other customers in the past. In other words, discuss how you have helped some customers reduce their attrition by "up to" 25 percent. This will establish the baseline to work up or down from. Next, you will want to establish a goal. Discuss with your prospect what his expectation is for the next three years and document the goal as the estimated value that you can deliver. Once you have come to agreement as to what the goal is and what your responsibility is, you have laid the foundation for returning each year and measuring your success.

Figure 3-6 shows a sample layout for the questions in a spreadsheet and the estimated goal for reducing customer attrition.

FIGURE 3-6

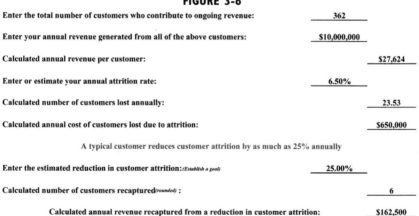

Enter the total number of customers who contribute to ongoing revenue:	362
Enter your annual revenue generated from all of the above customers:	$10,000,000
Calculated annual revenue per customer:	$27,624
Enter or estimate your annual attrition rate:	6.50%
Calculated number of customers lost annually:	23.53
Calculated annual cost of customers lost due to attrition:	$650,000
A typical customer reduces customer attrition by as much as 25% annually	
Enter the estimated reduction in customer attrition: *(Establish a goal)*	25.00%
Calculated number of customers recaptured *(rounded)* :	6
Calculated annual revenue recaptured from a reduction in customer attrition:	$162,500

SUMMARY

There are several key points in this chapter, and they all begin with the exercises in the previous chapter:

- Build your value inventory matrix as described in Chapter 2.

- Create your cost of status quo questions first.

- Create your pain-discovery questions after you have developed the cost of status quo questions.

- Be sure to ask the follow-on questions like, "What do you expect to happen in future years?" so that you are able to calculate future costs . . . and values.

- Identify and discuss the threshold for pain.

Creating a document (sales tool) that contains pain-discovery questions and cost of status quo questions is one of the basic tools of successful selling. The questions will force you to be consistent in your discovery, better organized, and better prepared when sitting down with a new prospect on a sales call. Regardless of the sales process or methodology that you currently employ, pain-discovery questions will play a major role in the discovery phase.

This chapter is designed to provide you with the information that you will need in order to ask the right questions to assess your prospect's pain and demonstrate the value that you can deliver to resolve the pain. In addition, by capturing and calculating cost and potential value, you are establishing the foundation for calculating your effect on your prospect's C-Suite metrics. Pain discovery drives consistent data gathering and professional appeal and differentiates you from your competition, helping to create the baseline data for communicating and selling to C-level executives.

A significant advantage of taking the time to complete this exercise is that next you are going to learn how to relate your value proposition and questions directly to the C-Suite metrics discussed in Chapter 1. The key is to be able to show the prospect's C-level executives how the value provided by your product or service affects one or more of the executives' closely watched financial metrics. Your value must reflect a change in their financial reports. To be able to make this connection and claim, you must be able to ask the questions that identify pain that drives them back to your solution. The questions must be quantitative in nature and reflect future costs as well.

Finally, this exercise will help you to uncover the pain that motivates a change. Remember, people make a change when the pain becomes too much to handle (the threshold for pain, or tipping point). When using these techniques, you will be able to not only identify pain, but extrapolate the pain over time and drive more responses to your effort.

In Chapter 4, we dive deeper into determining your value as it relates to C-Suite metrics. Before you move on, be sure that you have completed your value inventory, cost of status quo questions, pain-discovery questions, and future analysis questions.

CHAPTER

4

DETERMINING YOUR
VALUE TO THE C-SUITE

In the past, return on investment (ROI) was one of the determining factors that C-level executives used to make what- and when-to-buy decisions. In the business-to-business (B2B) world, it often came down to,
"What is the ROI, and when will we see it?" Times are different now; ROI
is less important. Why? Because, as one of my customers said, "Very few
organizations actually go back and measure the value (or nonvalue) that
sellers did or didn't deliver. ROI is just an overused and abused term." Each
year we ask hundreds of companies if they are measuring success after they
implement a new purchase, and the response reveals (as it did five years
ago) that less than 10 percent of the firms go back to check the ROI. This
lack of follow-up effort is one of the key reasons that true ROI measurements are going by the wayside.

That brings us to the question: What now? We have studied the buying patterns of corporations from $20 million to $750 million in annual
revenue and determined a major shift in who is involved in the buying

process. Across the board, there was a significant move toward more involvement by controllers, vice presidents of finance, and chief financial officers (CFOs). People at this level of financial management tend to use financial metrics to help them determine trends based on regular (usually monthly) analysis of the company's current financial position. They use these metrics to forecast earnings, profit, cash flow, days' sales outstanding (DSOs), and other such measures. In addition, they use these forecasts to determine budgets, make buying decisions, and establish strategic direction. A typical C-level executive will now know his company's current cash, line of credit, normal operating costs, and forecasted profit position at any point in time.

As a consultative sales professional, it is your responsibility to understand what metrics are being used and what they mean to the C-level executive who is using them to direct the corporate strategy. For example, if a prospect is deciding whether to invest in a backhoe or a software accounting system, the decision is basically between a revenue generator (the backhoe) and perhaps an added cost center (the accounting system). The analysis that is typically performed to make the why-buy decision is partially based on the effect on the C-Suite metrics (as defined in Chapter 1). This strategic buying decision takes into consideration many factors. These factors include cash position, debt-to-equity ratio, potential return on assets, lines of credit, credit rating, and DSOs, among others.

In this chapter, we will explore how these decisions are made and what you need to know (and do) to be a part of the decision-making equation as opposed to sitting on the sidelines watching.

HOW STRATEGIC BUYING DECISIONS ARE MADE

In the example just given, in which the decision is whether to buy a backhoe or an accounting system, pain plays an important role. An antiquated accounting system could lead to many measurable pains. For instance, if you are unable to get your billings out in a timely manner, this will lead to longer collection times, perhaps the need to borrow money, or, worse, the inability to collect receivables at all. Each of these pains is costly to the organization. If you have to borrow against your receivables, you are paying unnecessary interest and putting additional strain on your cash flow and the bottom line. In addition, you are losing interest income. If you are unable to make your payroll, your staff will leave, and your ability to deliver, invoice, and collect will most certainly decline.

Another problem that a company with an inadequate accounting system may face is the inability to manage the purchasing process. Construction companies, for example, must track all the materials they purchase for a job. They arrange delivery times, employ labor to install the materials when they arrive, pay the vendor for the materials, and invoice the owner for the percentage of work completed. This is an intricate process, and if any portion of the equation is off, the entire process costs the company money. If the labor shows up and the materials are not there, the labor costs for the job increase. If the materials are delivered and no labor shows up, the company is paying for materials to sit around. If the company pays an invoice too quickly without receiving a discount for early payment, then it is reducing cash flow. If it pays an invoice too late, it ends up paying fees for late payment. As you can see, each of these scenarios reveals the intricacies and pains in managing an accounting system.

On the backhoe side, most people would simply choose a backhoe because, "It will help us complete jobs sooner, generate additional income, and perhaps help us win bids because of the additional abilities that our organization is able to offer." However, the decision maker must also consider the maintenance, fuel, added labor cost, and depreciation. The backhoe is not a slam-dunk decision.

Each of these examples involves a potential increase in revenue, earnings, and likely profit. How does your buyer make the decision as to which asset to purchase? Does the company reduce costs and potentially increase revenues with a new accounting system, or does it increase revenue and take on costs with the purchase of a new backhoe?

Pain level plays a significant role in this decision. However, the concept of pain here is as it relates to the impact on the C-Suite metrics. In our accounting system example, the purchase is going to increase the operating costs of the organization. Depending upon how the company purchases the accounting system—capital outlay or SaaS (software as a service)—the impact will reflect differently on the C-Suite metrics and the financial reports.

On the other hand, a backhoe is likely to be a major asset purchase and will contribute to an increase in operating costs, labor, and upkeep. The C-Suite metrics impact to consider is the effect on cash flow, borrowing, depreciation, and additional operating costs for gas, oil, services, and repairs. All of these costs affect the bottom line (and the C-Suite metrics). They will affect net profit, debt-to-equity ratio, return on assets, earnings, and, of course, operating costs.

As the sales professional in either of these scenarios, do you really believe that features, benefits, and ROI are the metrics that the C-Suite is looking at in making the buying decision?

Here is another example: Consider the impact of expanding an operation. There are several decisions that must be made: number of staffers for the new location; cost for that staff; infrastructure costs, including phones, computers, printers, supplies, and so on; and then operating costs, such as utilities, maintenance, signage, and so on. If your product affects the operation, the C-Suite executives are considering more than the ROI. They are looking at ratios like debt to equity, return on assets, and return on equity in addition to the usual impact of ongoing operating costs and profit. If you are one of the vendors involved in selling an organization materials for a new operation, understanding the impact of your solution on the organization's strategic decision-making process is critical.

KEY POINT

You do not need to be a financial expert to use these techniques. You need to understand the C-Suite metrics and how your products and services will affect the financial levers that your prospect uses to make buying decisions.

IDENTIFYING YOUR IMPACT

Once again, the process begins with your value inventory. Chapter 2 discussed capturing and defining all the issues, pains, and goals that your prospects face each day. Chapter 3 showed how to convert your value inventory into questions that drive the pain-discovery part of your sales process. As part of discovery, you should identify the pain, capture the cost, calculate future effects, and gain agreement on the current and ongoing cost of the status quo.

This is typically the point in the sales process where you demonstrate your solution to your prospect's problem. Be sure to align your solution with the pains identified. In other words, demonstrate your product's value in relation to the pain you have discussed and agreed upon with the prospect. Too often, I see sales professionals who are so excited about their products that during the demonstration portion of the sale, they forget that they are solving problems and veer off the path into the "cool" stuff. Stay focused on the prospect's problem and your solution.

Discuss the effect that your solution will have on the prospect's pain in terms of financial impact. For example, suppose you are the accounting system sales professional from our previous example. If you demonstrate how your solution will enable the prospect to reduce the time it takes to enter and produce the monthly invoices, you are able to discuss more than the act of getting the billings out. You are able to discuss the potential reduction in labor cost, shortened time to collect on an invoice (DSOs), reduced need to borrow for cash flow purposes (lower interest payments), and potential revenue gains from interest income.

It is critical that you understand your solution's impact and its financial effects on an organization. In a C-Suite discussion, your conversation must include your product's potential impact on the following:

- Reduced payroll as a percentage of sales

- Increased revenue per employee

- Reduced operating costs

- Increased earnings

- Increased net profit

In addition, by reducing labor costs, you are able to affect 5 of the 10 C-Suite metrics defined in Chapter 1: earnings, operating costs, net and gross profit margin, payroll as a percentage of sales, and sales per employee. The impact on these 5 metrics can be measured almost immediately after the start-up period. The first billing cycle will produce results, and the impact will be reflected in the monthly financial reports.

Begin with the questions you have created that drive your prospects back to their pain and categorize the value that you are capable of delivering. In the previous example, we are discussing reducing and avoiding labor costs. Reductions come from fewer personnel needed to perform a task (create billings), and avoidances come from the fact that the company doesn't need to hire additional personnel to keep up with increased billings.

Table 4-1 gives some additional examples from the value inventory created in Chapter 2 for you to review. *Note:* When we first discussed the value inventory, we asked our CFO to list potential C-Suite impacts. This table is a more complete listing based on further discussion with our customers, prospects, and other CFOs who came to understand our value proposition. Continue to develop your value inventory over time as you communicate with financial experts in-house and with customers, prospects, and vendors.

KEY POINT

In each of the examples in Table 4-1, you will notice that the impact goes beyond the ROI. In the past, sales professionals sold based on features and benefits. Then, a few years ago, the transition to consultative selling and a more ROI-centric sale was required. Selling to the C-Suite is an extension of both of these methods. Your features drive value; the value drives the metrics.

Create your own charts or update your value inventory based on the value that you are capable of delivering. Remember to begin with your value inventory and create the value based on current cost and future cost questions to drive the prospect to understanding that the status quo is not free. Once you have defined your value as it relates to your prospect's issues, pains, and goals, then you can create the kind of C-Suite metric impact charts displayed here.

TABLE 4-1

Value Delivered	C-Suite Impact
Reduction in customer attrition. This drives a potential increase in revenue, because if your customers leave, you will lose revenue; by reducing the attrition, you are actually increasing revenue by recapturing revenue that was lost in the past.	• Increase in net profit • Increase in return on equity (ROE) • Increase in return on assets (ROA) • Increase in sales per employee • Reduction in payroll as a percentage of sales • Increase in earnings
Straight-up reduction in operating costs.	• Increase in profit • Increase in earnings • Reduction in operating costs
Reduction in transportation costs.	• Reduction in operating costs • Increase in profit • Increase in earnings

USING FINANCIAL REPORTS

When you use the C-Suite metrics to evaluate and discuss strategic purchases, your prospect has an opportunity to see the value delivered on a regular basis. Financial reports are run and distributed on at least a monthly basis; your short-term impact could be seen almost immediately on a cash flow analysis report and the balance sheet.

There are three primary financial reports included in every annual report: the income statement (often called the profit and loss statement, or P&L), the balance sheet, and the cash flow report. Each report provides information that you can use to better understand how a company is doing financially. You can also determine from these reports whether the company is growing or contracting and, of course, whether it is profitable. These are key factors in determining whether or not you want to engage in a sales process with this organization. If a company is in trouble financially, wouldn't it be nice to know that up front, before you engage? Let's briefly discuss each of the three reports that you will want to be familiar with.

Income Statement

Income statements are measures of the company's operating performance for a specified period of time. They span or bridge the gaps in time between consecutive balance sheet reports. The income statement (or P&L) simply captures income from all sources and subtracts expenses to give you a quick view of net income. If a backhoe generates income, it is reflected on the P&L. Accounting systems can track revenue by piece of equipment, so management can look at the immediate impact of the new purchase. However, the expense of owning the backhoe is reflected on the expense side of the income statement and must include payroll costs, service, and maintenance.

The balance sheet and the income statement reflect two different stories for the same organization. For example, just because a company made a "big profit" last year does not necessarily mean that it is liquid. A company may have reported significant net income, but still have a deficit in net worth. In other words, to find out how a company is really doing, you will need both the income statement and the balance sheet.

Finally, the income statement summarizes a company's operating results for a particular accounting period, and the results are reflected in the equity or net worth on the balance sheet.

Balance Sheet

The balance sheet portrays a company's financial position at a particular point in time. It includes assets (what the company owns), liabilities (what it owes), and what is left when you subtract one from the other, also known as net worth or equity. The balance sheet freezes the action, giving you the company's financial position at that moment in time.

Assets include balances in the company's bank account, receivables, and other items of value (like a backhoe) that it currently owns. Liabilities, on the other hand, include debt, payroll liabilities, and taxes owed. Shareholders' equity or net worth is generally calculated by subtracting liabilities from total assets. (It also reflects the equity figure for the previous period plus net income.) The balance sheet must balance assets with liabilities and equity.

The purchase decision to acquire a backhoe is easily seen on both sides of the ledger immediately (the cost of the backhoe and the revenue generated by the backhoe).

Cash Flow Report

The third report that publicly held companies make available to investors (and the public) is the cash flow report. It provides useful information about the inflow and outflow of cash that cannot be found on the balance sheet or the income statement. You will be able to see major cash outlays for capital purchases or debt reduction. (This would be of interest to a backhoe sales professional.) In addition, you will see major cash acquisitions. Remember that not all cash coming in is accounted for as revenue. Take a bank loan or line of credit, for example. A bank loan generates cash; however, it is not considered revenue, because no merchandise has been sold and no service has been delivered.

The bottom line is this: If you gain access to this information prior to your sales call with C-level executives, you are able to have a different conversation from those of your competition. You will know whether your prospect can afford to be talking with you before you walk in the door.

FINANCIAL REPORTS AND THE C-SUITE

Financial reports begin with revenue figures that come from merchandise sold and services delivered. If you are able to affect the amount of merchandise sold or services delivered to help increase revenue, then you will have an impact on the company's financial reports. Conversely, expenses on financial reports include rent, payroll, interest payments, fines, depreciation, and other such items. When your value helps a prospect reduce these expenses, once again you have an impact on the financial reports.

This point may seem obvious, but it is rarely used or discussed at the C-level by sales professionals or management. The reason you went through the exercise of defining your value (creating a value inventory) and correlating it with the C-Suite metrics is to gain this knowledge and understanding of your impact on the financial reports used to make strategic buying decisions. Every line of your value inventory tells the story of how you can possibly affect the balance sheet, income statement, and/or cash flow statement.

> **KEY POINT**
> When you have reviewed the financial reports in advance, you are in a position to discuss your solution, your value, and your impact.

RESEARCHING YOUR PROSPECT'S FINANCIAL INFORMATION

There is no substitute for doing your homework. The more you know about a prospect, the better off you will be when dealing with C-level executives. There are many ways to obtain the data you need before you meet with a CFO, CEO, or others for the first time. If the prospect company is publicly held, you have free access to its annual report, 10-K reports, and letters and notes from the president to the shareholders, and, of course, you can look up what the analysts think of the company. You can sit in on the company's quarterly earnings calls or simply contact its investor relations department and ask for a packet of information. As a backup plan, you can always buy a single share of stock. With that single share, you are entitled to the same information as an investor who has thousands of shares.

If the prospect is not a publicly held company, however, you have to resign yourself to using other means. There are many pay-for-information sites, such as Hoovers (www.hoovers.com), Dun & Bradstreet (DNB; www.dnb.com), and one of my favorites, InsideView (www.insideview.com), to name a few. These sites have data on executives' names, phone numbers, and education; the company's revenue; and other such information. In fact, InsideView will track new articles on accounts and send you a daily update on where they appear and what is being said in the marketplace. Check out www.whyjohnnycantsell.com for a more complete list of sites that you can visit to do background research on public and private corporations.

In preparation for a meeting I had with one C-level executive, I did a quick lookup on InsideView and found out that he had gone to the same college as I did a few years later. We immediately bonded through a discussion about a particular professor. You can use sites like Jigsaw (www.jigsaw.com) or ZoomInfo (www.zoominfo.com) to find names, e-mail addresses, and direct phone numbers. Don't forget about social networking sites, too, like LinkedIn (www.linkedin.com) or Facebook (www.facebook.com), for assistance in gaining access to an executive. There are so many choices that you may want to try out different ones on a short-term basis before settling on any particular product or service.

Remember, the key to a successful research site is the amount of data that it can give you access to that you cannot get in the public domain without a great deal of effort. In other words, by doing a Google search, you will be able to gather a lot of information on a company. You must first ask if it is worth the time it takes to do your own research or if you should pay a service to do it for you. Try both and make your own decision going forward. However you go about doing it, it is necessary to obtain background information before you meet with C-level executives.

One last point is that if the company is public, the executive profiles are a matter of public record. If the company is not public, you may want to first obtain executives' names from the company's web site and do an Internet search for the names for some background information. This effort is free!

THE FINANCIAL MANAGER'S RESPONSIBILITIES IN AN ORGANIZATION

It is important to realize the key responsibilities of the financial manager in any organization. Large corporations typically have a vice president of finance, a controller, and possibly a treasurer as well. Small companies generally have only one level of finance, and it is managed by the CFO. Regardless of the size of the organization, these basic responsibilities apply to all in the finance group:

- Planning and budgeting

- Provision of capital

- Cash management

- Accounting functions

- Protecting assets

- Managing investors

- Handling complete tax requirements
  (all government regulations)

It is important to note that in these more stringent economic times, the CFO is often called upon to provide other executives (C-level and VP-level) in the organization with advice on budgeting, planning, and purchase decision making. As a consultative sales professional, you should know this and use this information when talking with department heads and other nonfinancial VPs or C-level executives. Simply ask your inside financial coach what role the finance department will play in the decision-making process.

SUMMARY

Your product value must be intricately tied to metrics that the C-Suite uses to determine the best strategic buying decisions it can make. Before any organization makes a major purchasing decision, there is analysis by someone in a finance position of metrics and ratios like cash flow, depreciation, return on equity (ROE), debt to equity, cash position, and earnings before interest, taxes, depreciation, and amortization (EBITDA). Knowing and understanding your value and its impact on the C-Suite metrics will provide you with insight into the buyer's thought process. Your ability to articulate your position and impact will create a gap between you and your closest competitor.

> ### KEY POINT
> A transportation vendor once approached a car rental agency about saving cost by purchasing and licensing its vehicles in a state where the cost of registering and licensing them was considerably less expensive, then transporting them to other locations to be used. When the agency realized the impact of the cost reductions on its financial reports, it was an easy (and very quick) decision. If you understand the impact a decision can make on your prospect's financial reports (cash flow statement, balance sheet, and income statement), you are miles ahead of your competitors who are still selling features and benefits.

There is a financial vocabulary you will want to learn that includes items on the balance sheet and income statement and their function and purpose, in addition to the C-Suite metrics and why they are important to the financial analyst using them to make strategic decisions. Learning what metrics an organization is using will help you understand the health of that organization. If you are aware of an organization's cash position, debt-to-equity ratio, and current plans for expansion or contraction, then you are able to make an informed decision on whether to pursue a sales opportunity or not. If your sale will take more than a few months, it is worth the time and effort to dig deep into an organization before you start the sales process. If the organization is not in a position to purchase, you are wasting your time. On the other hand, isn't it good to know if the organization is in a position to purchase?

There are many ways to research an organization's health. Publicly held companies publish most of the answers you need on their web site in the form of letters from the president to shareholders, annual reports, 10-K filings, and more. You also have the option of sitting in on a quarterly earnings call with analysts. Usually the CFO will give a state of the company report, too. Your challenge comes when you are trying to research a company this is privately held. In that case, the data are not so readily available. There are several pay-for-information web sites (like Hoovers, InsideView, or ZoomInfo) that do the research for you. As an alternative, you can use sites like Jigsaw to get a name, phone number, and e-mail address and do your own research on the Internet. Look for articles, case study comments, white papers, or research and you can make your own determination as to whether a company is a good prospect to pursue.

Take the time to understand a corporation's financial structure. Remember, large organizations disperse financial decision making throughout the company. You don't need to work from the top. In large corporations, find the decision maker within the group you are working with. Ask your inside finance coach about the financial structure early in the sales process. Discuss the level of input that the financial group will have on the buying decision.

Finally, it is your responsibility to:

- Understand the C-Suite metrics.

- Identify your impact on those metrics and the financial reports.

- Create value and impact charts.

- Learn to read a financial statement, a 10-K, and an annual report.

- Get to know the prospect's financial structure.

- Learn to interpret the language used by financial experts.

Be sure to create your value inventory, develop your pain-discovery questions, and correlate your value with the impact on the metrics. The more financial information you are able to collect and compare, the better equipped you will be to close a sales opportunity. If you are out there talking about features and benefits and ROI, then you are going to be left out of the buying decision process.

In Chapter 5, we will cover how to use the information you have collected throughout your sales process. In addition, we will introduce you to a new tool that enables you to compare your prospect's C-Suite metrics to normal and customary metrics for the industry. Imagine having the ability to compare your prospect's net profit margin, for example, to the industry norm and then have a discussion of your product's (or service's) impact on net profit margin.

CHAPTER 5

COLLECTING INFORMATION DURING YOUR SALES PROCESS

This chapter reveals how to collect the necessary data and build confidence in your ability to discuss the results with C-level executives. Put away your fears and get a better understanding of what your discussion with the CEO and CFO is all about. We cover questioning techniques, information gathering (sources of information), and a typical sales call on a CFO, CEO, or other C-level professionals.

Preparation is the key to success in a C-level sales call. This book is not about how to open the doors to the C-Suite. It is about how to have an intelligent conversation regarding the effect of your product or service on the senior executives' most important metrics and how to win when you are there. For more help with opening the door, see Jill Konrath's book *Selling to Big Companies* (Dearborn Publishing, 2006), or Anthony Parinello's book *Selling to VITO,* 3rd ed. (Adams Media Corporation, 1999).

THE STAGES OF THE SALES PROCESS

At each stage of your sales process, there are tools required to identify pain, gather critical information (discovery), and make certain recommendations (proposal) based on your research and your potential value to the prospect. For the sake of this discussion, let's begin with a simple sales process. Outlined here is a basic method of qualifying prospects; identifying their issues, pains, and goals through a discovery phase; capturing and calculating the current and future (ongoing) cost of the status quo; presenting a solution; proposing an investment; and then working through the contract to get to a close. (See Figure 5-1.)

FIGURE 5-1

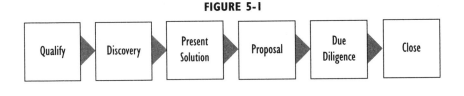

I. QUALIFY

You must begin your sales journey by qualifying your prospect from a group of target accounts. Developing good qualifying questions will establish the groundwork during the discovery phase of the sales process. Be sure you do not confuse the discovery phase with the qualifying stage. Qualifying a prospect should come down to only a few factors:

- Does the prospect meet your minimum marketing criteria?

- Does she have the means to purchase from you?

- Is there a motivation to buy?

Meet Marketing Criteria

This is the simplest qualifier. You must establish a minimum and maximum size organization to sell to. The qualifier can be by revenue, number of staff members, or some other quantitative measurement. For example, QuickBooks focuses on small- to medium-size businesses, whereas SAP focuses on major corporations. They each know their market, and they rarely compete against each other. You, too, must first define your market criteria.

Means to Purchase

This does not necessarily mean that the prospect has a budget within which it must work. Many purchases are made outside of a budget. Means is simply this: Is the prospect capable of buying from you? Research will help you answer this question. Look for articles, recent purchases, hiring notices, and credit checks. Remember what you learned in the previous chapter about the ability to purchase from you.

Motivation to Buy

The motivation to buy is a bit more subjective. Often it takes a discussion of a high-level pain and what the prospect wants to do about it. The problem here is that motivations change rapidly, so you need to make sure that you continue to "stoke the fire" during discovery to help the prospect keep feeling the pain. Once you have determined that the prospect is qualified, you should quickly move on to the discovery phase of your sales process.

2. DISCOVERY

During discovery, a lot of things are happening at once. You are trying to understand what the decision-making process is going to be, the estimated budget that the prospect has to spend, the key stakeholders you must get to know, what reasons might prevent the prospect from buying from you, at what point the prospect wants to realize your value, and, of course, who is involved in the actual decision-making process and what are their issues, pains, and goals. In addition, you must identify pain, capture and calculate current and future cost, and discuss the threshold for pain.

At the same time, the prospect is trying to get a better understanding of your organization and who you are. He is concerned that you cannot meet his needs, or that you don't understand his issues, pains, and goals. He is assessing the risk of dealing with you and your organization. Because there are always some projects that fail, risk plays a major role in the decision-making process. Your responsibility is to help mitigate that risk by making your prospect feel comfortable with you and your organization. This is achieved by presenting yourself and your company as organized professionals. There used to be a saying, "No one was ever fired for buying IBM." This was because of IBM's projected image and its ability to help a prospect feel as though IBM will always be there to help. IBM people would show up in their blue suits and white shirts ready to help customers in any way they could . . . for a significant fee, of course.

The discovery phase is one of the most critical phases of the sales process. Too often, sales professionals "gloss over" the discovery phase and move right on to the demonstration or presentation phase, hoping to hit on an issue or a hot button. This is commonly called the "show up and throw up" method of selling. We are proposing that you spend more time in discovery than in presentation. Discovery is where you establish the foundation for using the C-Suite metrics to sell.

KEY POINT

The pain-discovery questions that you created earlier and that you ask at this point in the sales process are the foundation for building your dashboard and your business case. Each time your prospect responds to a quantitative-based question, she is adding more value to your solution. Remember, you must ensure that your questions first identify pain and then—through discussion—draw your prospect back to you for a solution.

Your pain-discovery questions, your questioning process, and the data that you collect lay the foundation for a better understanding of your prospect's pain and threshold for pain, and for building your business case. You will gain strategic insight into the financial levers that your prospects wish to move. For example, if a company is trying to expand its operations, but does not have the cash, perhaps its strategy is to lease or "expense" its expansion. It would serve no purpose for you to meet with such a company and try to *sell* it major assets like copiers or a phone system. Clearly its strategy would be to lease the assets.

When you use the primary discovery questions that you created earlier, be sure to get agreement from your prospects that they are in fact experiencing the pain. Then move on to the follow-up questions on capturing and calculating the current cost of the status quo. Again, get agreement on the cost, and then move on to calculating the ongoing future cost of the status quo. Be sure you get agreement on this, too. Very few people buy when they don't feel pain.

The ongoing cost calculations are the setup for the threshold-for-pain discussion. You want to create an "aha moment" where your prospect says, "I have had enough of this pain, and I am going to do something about it." There are many reasons why people buy products and services. The most common by far is the human emotion that says, "I have reached my tipping point, and I am going to solve my problem." Think about it in this way: A person with tennis elbow, for example, will take ibuprofen to "mask" the pain and provide temporary relief. He could go on this way for years. At some point, however, the person will either stop doing the activity or have surgery to repair the problem and end the pain. Corporations think similarly. They are likely to mask the pain for years before investing in a solution. Timing is crucial, and knowing the threshold point is a key to success.

Finally, as you work through the discovery phase of the sales process, keep in mind your value as it relates to the C-Suite metrics. As you work through the discovery questions and begin to calculate costs, be aware that each answer you receive has an impact on the prospect's key financial levers or C-Suite metrics. For example, during your pain-discovery call, you discuss that your prospect "needs to reduce overall labor costs." You should immediately realize your effect on the C-Suite metrics. Reducing the labor costs will:

- Reduce payroll as a percentage of sales

- Increase sales per employee

- Increase net profit

- Reduce operating costs

You know this because your value inventory told you of the impact on the C-Suite from labor cost reductions. When you spend the time to understand your prospects' issues, pains, and goals, and to understand your value and value proposition as it relates to the C-Suite metrics, your questioning process can give you critical information on how to plan your sales attack and begin building your business case. Your value inventory should have captured every possible reason that someone would buy from you. Armed with this information, you have an advantage because during the discovery phase, you will know the pain, the stakeholders, the desired outcome, the solution, and the C-Suite impact. (Refer to your value inventory.)

Early in the sales process is where you are able to gather the most information. Your questions will help you identify pain and zero in on areas where your products or services will be most effective. Take the time to understand the pain. We find that prospects are typically more open during this bonding-and-discovery stage than later down the line, when you are supposed to be proving your value and proposing a solution. Figure 5-2 shows how we see the exchange of information and the level of importance to the prospect during a typical sales process.

Notice that during the qualifying stage and the discovery stage, your prospect's pains are most important. You are able to gather the most information at this point. Also, notice how your solution becomes more important as the sales process continues over time through the presentation phase. We will add additional lines to this chart later so that you are able to get the complete picture as to what is going on in your prospect's mind.

FIGURE 5-2

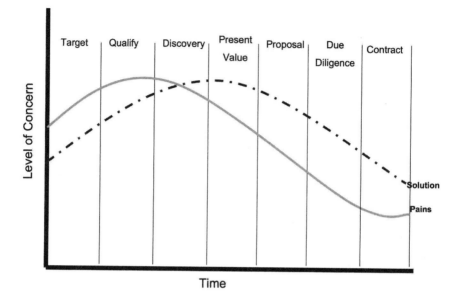

Discovery Data Collection

We need to back up a little and look at the preparation required to capture the data needed to get to the C-Suite effect. Each sales call you make on a prospect should be carefully planned out. There is no substitution for preparation. We suggest that you create questions that will help you negotiate information and at the same time provide your prospects with comfort through the fact you understand their pain and can help them. This isn't always easy if your prospect:

- Doesn't understand and agree to the problem

- Has no idea of the current cost of the problem

- Is reluctant to provide you with critical information

Let's take a look at each excuse your prospect has for not answering your discovery questions.

Prospect Doesn't Understand or Agree on the Problem. In this case, the value inventory and primary discovery preparation are really important. Having a list of key questions ready that drive your prospect back to your value will:

- Help you uncover and identify pain (sometimes hidden pain).

- Gain agreement on pain.

- Establish the current and ongoing cost.

When you are trying to uncover pain, it is important that you develop questions that will help your prospects discover issues, pains, and goals that they may not realize they have. In addition, you must be able to equate or relate the pain to the effect on prospects' financial levers. For example, here are some common sample questions that you might ask a prospect during discovery:

- Are increased labor costs causing a strain on your *operating expenses*?

- Is your inability to get billings out on time forcing you to extend your *days' sales outstanding (DSOs)* and borrow funds for cash flow?

- Is customer attrition affecting your *net profit*?

Table 5-1 is a C-Suite impact table that identifies the baseline pain and captures the potential movement on the prospect's financial levers.

Once you are armed with this information during your discovery call, your conversation will take a path that very few other vendors will be able to match. When a prospect doesn't understand the issues, your questions and follow-up conversation as to the financial impact of ignoring the problem will help crystallize the pain and establish a foundation for discussing the threshold.

TABLE 5-1

Pain Question	Pain Captured	Potential C-Suite Metric
Are increased labor costs causing a strain on operating costs?	Increased labor costs	• Operating cost • Net profit • Payroll as a percent of sales • Sales per employee • Earnings
Is your inability to get billings out on time forcing you to borrow and extend your DSOs?	Frustration of not getting billings out in a timely manner	• DSOs • Net profit • Operating costs • Earnings
Is customer attrition affecting your net profit?	Loss of customers	• Net profit • Sales per employee • Earnings • Payroll as a percent of sales • Return on assets (ROA) • Return on equity (ROE)

KEY POINT

Remember, people buy when they reach a point at which they cannot accept the cost (pain) any longer.

Finally, by creating your discovery questions in advance and building a C-Suite impact table like Table 5-1, you are able to:

- Identify and uncover the real pain.

- Gain a better understanding of how the C-Suite metrics are going to affect your prospect's financial levers.

If you have completed your value inventory or have been in business for any length of time and have a customer base, then you have a keen understanding of the problems that you are able to solve. Your success depends upon your ability to create questions that capture the data (pain/cost) that you need if you are to understand the value (solution) that you are capable of delivering. You, of course, must deliver that value if you are to be successful.

Remember, your questions uncover issues, pains, and goals and create uneasiness in your prospect's mind. Prospects need to "feel" the pain. Your goal at this stage is simple: Uncover and identify pain, gain confirmation from your prospect on the pain, and help calculate the current and ongoing cost of the status quo.

Prospect Has No Idea of the Cost of the Problem. This is a common problem in every sales situation. Very few decisions to buy are made if a prospect doesn't feel pain, so this is obviously a critical piece of information that you must collect and get agreement on from your prospect. There are several strategies that you may want to consider:

- Create questions to get to current cost.

- Use research to estimate current cost.

- Dissect public information (annual report, 10-K, Dun & Bradstreet [D&B] report, Hoovers report, and so on).

There is a questioning technique that you can use to calculate current cost. It is based on the idea that if you break pain down into smaller pieces, then put all these pieces together for your prospect, you can arrive at the destination you set out for in the beginning. Let's say you are a prospect who is interested in improving your sales training program. If I asked you, "Do you know what your return on training dollars spent is?" would you know the answer? Probably not, but if I asked you:

- "How much do you spend (budget) annually on training?"

- "How many sales professionals do you train with that budget?"

- "What is the annual revenue that these sales professionals generate?"

I could calculate the dollar return on each dollar spent on sales training. (See Figure 5-3.)

FIGURE 5-3

Enter your current annual training budget:	$350,000
Enter the number of sales professionals who are trained annually from this budget:	24
Calculated annual training budget spent per sales professional:	$14,583
Enter the annual revenue generated by these sales professionals:	$15,000,000
Calculated average revenue per sales professional:	$625,000
Dollar return for each dollar spent on training:	$42.86

In the example in Figure 5-3, we broke down the main answer we were looking for into a series of questions that we knew our prospect would know the answers to, then performed some very simple math. We divided the annual budget by the number of sales professionals. Next, we divided the annual revenue by the number of sales professionals. And finally, we divided the average revenue per sales professional by the average training dollar spent per sales professional to come up with the dollar return for each dollar spent on training.

Why is this calculation a key concern if you are trying to sell the prospect a training program? Because by increasing revenue, the prospect is able to increase the dollar return on each dollar spent on training the sales force. If your value proposition was to help new hires become more productive sooner by training them to sell better, then your point of increasing the dollar return on dollars spent on training is a valid point. Your approach is to attack the financial lever. In addition, the prospect will be able to increase profit, increase earnings, improve revenue per employee, and reduce operating costs. All of these are possible with an increase in the amount of revenue that a new hire sells.

Let's look at another example of how to get the answers when your prospect has no idea of the cost of the problem.

Customer attrition is always a painful subject. One of our clients looked at the cost to replace a lost customer. Using math to determine how much is spent annually on new customer acquisitions, this client simply multiplied the cost per new customer by the number of customers lost each year (see the example in Figure 5-4). If the client had asked, "What is the cost to replace a lost customer?" we seriously doubt that the prospect would have known the answer. However, the fact that our client could capture information that the prospect does know and provide valuable feedback is a major advantage over the competition.

FIGURE 5-4

Enter your annual marketing budget:	$2,000,000
Enter the percentage of marketing budget dedicated to new customer acquisition:	85.00%
Enter the number of new customers acquired annually through customer acquisition:	400
Calculated budget spent on new customer acquisition:	$1,700,000
Enter number of customer lost annually due to attrition:	72
Calculated cost per new customer acquired:	$4,250
Calculated annual cost to replace lost customers:	$306,000

The $306,000 is an annual cost to replace the 72 lost customers. Depending upon the value proposition to solve this issue, you may affect earnings, net profit, and operating costs. Be sure to capture cost and look at your value as it relates to moving your prospects' financial levers.

KEY POINT

If you are unable to get the information you need, break up the questions into pieces that your prospect will know, and then reassemble them using math to get to the cost basis you need to help the prospect feel the pain.

Prospect Is Reluctant to Provide Critical Information. There is an old saying in sales: "Buyers are liars!" The worst part is that they usually don't even realize that they are lying.

Given this fact, our feeling is that if certain prospects are unwilling to answer your quantitative-based questions, then they are not very good prospects. If a prospect is unwilling to spend the time with you and provide the critical information that you need to make a genuine, sincere recommendation, then we believe you should move on to another sales opportunity. However, if you insist that this is a good prospect and you want to pursue it, what follows is our suggestion when you are being stonewalled.

Your mission is to create your value inventory, then create the questions that identify pain and drive your prospects back to you for help. Prior to executing a process of pain discovery, you will need to establish some default baseline averages for the discovery questions you have created. We believe you can establish these default baseline answers by first looking into your existing customer base.

Your Current Customer Base. We strongly recommend that you establish some default baseline answers to your pain-discovery questions, by size of prospective organization. Use the questions you have built to identify pain and return to your current customer base to ask what their answers would be to the pain-discovery questions. Once you have accumulated some baseline averages, document them for your entire team to use when they need to "precomplete" a discovery questionnaire.

Once you have precompleted a questionnaire, confirm or validate the answers with your prospect. In other words, if the prospect won't give you her own answers, ask her to adjust the answers you have entered from your own customer base.

In our earlier examples of pain-discovery questions, we discussed "customer attrition," or "cost to replace a customer who has decided to leave you." Here are examples of questions you can ask your customer to help you establish the baseline for the questionnaire:

- Mr. Customer, one of the goals when you purchased from us was to reduce your customer attrition rate. Can you tell me what the average attrition rate was *before you implemented our solution*?

- Ms. Customer, we discussed (and calculated) the cost to acquire a new customer to replace one who has turned over or left you. Can you tell me what percentage of your customer base turns each year?

These questions are valid if your solution was discussed and implemented over the past couple of years. You are simply reminding an existing customer of your value proposition and asking what the baseline problem looked like before the customer implemented your solution. (Look at this as an opportunity to bond with an existing customer.)

Here is another example. To figure out the revenue of a company that is not publicly held and is unwilling to disclose it, we like to use the figure $203,000 for revenue per employee. For example, if a company won't tell you its revenues, ask, "How many employees do you have on your payroll?" Next, multiply the number of employees by $203,000 and you should be within 10 to 15 percent of the total revenue. Most organizations will reveal their employee count without much pushback. Or you can research this through D&B or Hoovers. Keep in mind that this is just a simple technique to use that will get you close to actual revenues. You will still need validation down the line to complete your business case.

As we noted earlier, with publicly held companies, pretty much all of the financial information you require is available for the asking. Get a copy of the company's annual report from investor relations, and it will tell you company revenue, forecast, trends, profits, earnings per share, and—one of our favorite sections—"management's discussion and analysis." This section is where management is required to discuss all past and future conditions and uncertainties that may materially affect the business. To obtain a copy of an annual report, our favorite resources are the following:

- EDGAR is located under the "Filings & Forms" section at www.sec.gov.

- Public Register's annual report service allows you to request an annual report and will process your request within 24 hours: www.prars.com.

- The company's web site is also useful. Look under "investor relations."

Industry Norm. We came across a great web site on financial metrics (C-Suite metrics) norms by industry from *Inc.* magazine. The web site is http://www.inc.com/profitability-report/index.html. Please note that the data is supplied by Sageworks, Inc., www.sageworksbenchmarking.com. The web site displays financial metric norms for 19 different industries, including mining, construction, retail, and management services, among others. It gives you the normal range for metrics like earnings before interest, taxes, depreciation, and amortization (EBITDA); net and gross margin; debt-to-equity ratio; return on assets; return on equity; and accounts receivable DSOs. There are about 20 different metrics divided by industry that you can examine for free.

This web site (tool) should become an important part of your sales arsenal. In earlier chapters, we spent a lot of time discussing the importance of research. This web site is an additional opportunity to capture information that you can use in your C-level conversation. It also gives you a baseline to determine whether your prospect is above or below the industry norm.

If your prospect is outside of the normal range, then you have valuable information that C-level executives will want to know. For example, according to *Inc.* magazine's web site, the average number of accounts receivable days outstanding, or DSOs, for a professional services firm is 35 days. Let's assume first that you have a product that reduces DSOs, and next that your research has revealed that your prospect is sitting at 50 days. You know from your value inventory that your solution can reduce DSOs by up to 25 percent. This is where you can connect the dots and have a frank discussion on helping this prospect get back within the normal range for DSOs for a professional services firm. Moving prospects into a normal range or keeping them performing better than the normal range will almost certainly make you a trusted advisor.

This tool will help you uncover and identify pain that your prospects probably won't even realize that they have. Use this information as you work through the discovery phase of the sales process.

Before we move on to proving your value, we want to caution you about going too far with your discovery efforts. Unfortunately, many buyers are not really buyers; all they are looking for is an education or a company to use to compare to what they really want to buy. These fishing expeditions are very costly and time-consuming. Don't consult for free! As you work through your questions, be aware that the prospect may be trying to take advantage of you and your knowledge.

3. PRESENT SOLUTION

In our sample process defined earlier, once you have completed your discovery phase by identifying pain and determining the current and ongoing cost of that pain, it is time to prove your value and present a solution.

You must take the information that you have collected and focus on presenting a solution that will resolve your prospects' pain, have a positive impact on their C-suite metrics, and provide a win-win environment for everyone involved in the process. Too many sales professionals focus on their solution, ignoring the specific data that they collected during the discovery phase. The answers that you get during the discovery phase lay the foundation for the proof presentation. Remember to refer to your value inventory for key information on your solution and its C-Suite impact. During your proof presentation, be sure to focus on the issues discussed, the pains identified, and the value that you are capable of delivering. We can lose to the status quo because we don't put enough emphasis on the actual pains that we identified and the long-term cost of the status quo. When demonstrating your value, always confirm the pain, the cost of that pain, and the value of your solution.

Many sales opportunities are lost because the prospect's perception of the value received does not exceed the investment required. When you put too much emphasis on the solution and not enough on the financial impact, you leave the interpretation up to the prospect. Enable your prospect to participate in the value-estimation process. This technique is really quite simple; it is done through questions. Here is an example:

> YOU: "I want to be sure I am demonstrating what you need to see in order to make an informed decision. I am referring to the questions we discussed earlier. When we talked before, you mentioned that customer attrition is a problem for you. Is this still correct?"

> PROSPECT: "Yes, it is."

> YOU: "Thank you. In addition to customer attrition, we talked about your spending $1.7 million a year on prospect-generation marketing programs. Is that still correct, too?"

> PROSPECT: "Yes, that is true."

> YOU: "Looking at the numbers we agreed on reveals that you spend $4,250 per new customer acquired. So that means that to replace the 72 customers lost, you must spend an additional $306,000. Is that also true?"

> PROSPECT: "It seems high, but I guess it's true."

> YOU: "Allow me to show you how we can help you reduce your customer attrition and in turn use the money spent to replace lost customers on acquiring new customers."

The C-Suite effect is a key factor in the presentation in that you must identify the problem, present the solution, and then discuss the impact.

The discussion that follows is the most important part of the presentation. This discussion must include the prospects' buy-in that:

* They do in fact have the problem defined.

* The problem is costing them X dollars.

* The ongoing cost is going to be Y dollars.

* You have a solution, and it fulfills their needs.

Once you go through this process on each of the defined issues, you are ready to discuss the impact on the C-Suite metrics. However, remember that this must be done at the right level within your prospect's organization.

Another reason for getting a no-buy decision is selling at the wrong level in an organization. It is fine to collect the data for your questionnaire from multiple midlevel management sources. However, the C-Suite metrics are important only to a decision maker. Remember this fact when you are discussing your impact on things like operating costs or net profit. If you are not getting a response showing interest and recognition of your impact's importance, a big red flag should go up because you are talking to the wrong people within this organization. Your impact should be a key factor in the strategic decision-making process.

Business Case Preparation

I obviously can't teach you how to demonstrate your value; however, I can teach you how to present your value in the most favorable light. If you have gone through the steps to understanding your value in the earlier chapters, then you are positioned to create a business case that is compelling and will help you persuade your prospects that you can resolve their problem and return value that will positively affect their financial levers.

In the next two chapters, we are going to go into detail on how to present your C-Suite metrics findings on a financial dashboard and how to create a compelling business case. First, we want to make sure that you are prepared.

Capture and Document Baseline

From Chapter 1 until now, we have focused on several key points. They are:

- Create your value inventory.

- Develop questions to identify pain and capture current cost.

- Extrapolate the cost over three to seven years (threshold for pain).

- Demonstrate your value (proof presentation).

- Discuss the impact of your value as it relates to the C-Suite metrics.

Each of these steps is crucial to developing a high-quality business case. In addition, each step will help generate the data that will be used on your financial dashboard and in your business case documents. Here is a short description of the data from each of these steps that you will need to document prior to building your financial dashboard and your business case.

Value Inventory. Your value inventory contains the key to the C-Suite metrics. Remember that each line tells a story of the value that you are capable of delivering. Each line also tells you the C-Suite impact that you can use on your financial dashboard and in your business case. Compare the value areas that you captured from your prospect and note the C-Suite impacts that you have documented in your value inventory.

Discovery Questions. The basis for your business case comes in the form of the answers to your primary discovery questions that you collected. Be sure you document the answers so that you are able to repeat the questions and the answers on your dashboard and in your business case documents.

Threshold for Pain. Three to seven years of cost and value analysis is the basis for helping your prospect realize that maintaining the status quo is not free. This is a key part of reducing the number of no-decision losses that you experience. In addition, these calculations will prompt the threshold-for-pain discussion that you must have to better understand *when* your prospect will purchase. Be sure to document the three- to seven-year extrapolation.

Proof Presentation. This is your opportunity to confirm and validate the pains and cost of pains identified during the discovery phase. In addition, you are able to establish and document goals based on the value that you can deliver after demonstrating your proof. In other words, once you prove that you can deliver a solution, you will want to discuss the value of that solution and determine a goal by which to measure your success.

Value Impact and the C-Suite. When you have proven your value in the proof presentation and discussed the value of your solution, your next discovery effort must be establishing the status quo for the C-Suite metrics. For example, the only way to discuss your impact on net profit is to understand what the prospect's current revenue and net profit margin are. The same is true for all C-Suite metrics. You must establish the status quo and then apply your impact based on the goals defined during the proof presentation.

4. DUE DILIGENCE

One of my favorite sales trainers is David Sandler. His method is based around the idea that as you complete one phase of your sales process, you should close the door on it and never return. In other words, once you complete the discovery phase of the process, you should never return to do it again. Due diligence is the part of the sales process where your customers will check up on you to help mitigate the risk of doing business with you. They will probably check references and credit reports and maybe even pull a D&B report on you.

At this point in the sales process, your prospect's risk if he purchases from you is at the highest level. He has all your information, including a business case, a proposal, and references. He is ready to make a decision, but he still wonders: Are you a high-quality vendor? Can you really deliver as promised? As you can see from Figure 5-5, risk continues to rise as the prospect engages more with you as a vendor.

FIGURE 5-5

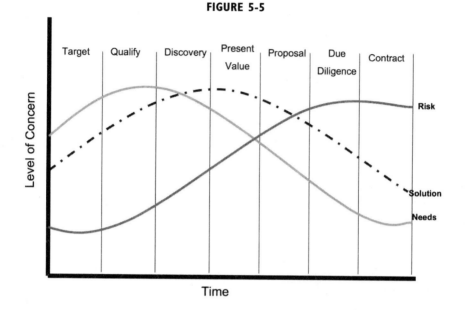

Time

In selling to the C-Suite, when you submit your business case and proposal, you must be prepared to provide your prospect with information that will mitigate the risk of doing business with you. Buying is based on vendor value, financial impact, and the ability to prove that you can deliver the business case.

As you work through the exercises in building your value inventory, creating your discovery questions, and developing your business case, the experience of your current customers must shed light on the value that you are capable of delivering. There is comfort in knowing that your organization is capable of delivering value. Be sure to capture your customer experiences and share them with your prospect to help mitigate the risk of doing business with you.

5. CLOSE

Skilled sales professionals can qualify a prospect, uncover pain, recommend a solution, and bring a sale to a close. Each step in the sales process requires different tools and different skills. We have helped you to create tools to identify pain, capture and calculate current cost, estimate your value, and create a high-quality business case. These tools are the foundation for success when selling to the C-Suite.

When each step is executed properly, with validation from your prospect, the close should happen naturally. Unfortunately, it doesn't always just "happen." When you are using sales tools that capture and document pain and value, it is obvious sooner when to walk away from bad deals. In addition, it is also easier to bring a sale to a close.

SUMMARY

Chapter 5 should have prompted you to think more about your sales process and how to capture the data you need if you are to prepare for a C-level conversation. Your discussion of the C-Suite metrics is set up by the data that you collect during discovery. We have provided you with concepts that you can adopt and implement right away. They include:

- Techniques for qualifying your prospect

- Performing discovery with an eye toward your impact on the financial levers

- Obtaining prospect data even when they are not available

- How to capture cost after you identify pain

- A new tool to compare C-Suite metrics by industry

- How to prove your value and use the pain threshold as a tool

- How to prepare for a meeting in the C-Suite

There is no substitute for preparation. C-level executives expect you to be knowledgeable and prepared. They want to know that you are able to understand their business and strategic goals, and can offer insight into their issues and pains. Using tools like Hoovers, InsideView, or Jigsaw enables you to do research long before you ever walk in the prospect's door.

Your sales process must include qualifying your prospect. This book assumes that you already have a qualified prospect and are ready for the discovery phase of the sales process. Your questioning process must include a basic understanding of the prospect's pain, the current and ongoing cost of that pain, and the potential financial impact that your solution may have. Once you have a solid understanding of your prospect's issues, you can then address your impact on the C-Suite metrics. Keep in mind, however, that just because you have a solution does not mean that you understand the financial impact of your solution. This leap must be made by using the last column of your value inventory and applying the appropriate calculations.

Once you have proved that you can resolve the problem, you need to estimate and calculate your value and then use it as the baseline for impact analysis. In other words, you need to capture and calculate your value, capture and calculate your prospect's current C-Suite metrics, and then apply your value and calculate the ratio change based on the value estimates delivered.

We introduced you to a tool that you can obtain for free from *Inc.*'s web site, a tool developed and maintained by Sageworks, that will help you compare your prospect's current C-Suite metrics to an industry norm. This information can be used to compare your prospect's current situation to a "standard" in the market. If your prospect is outside the norm, your conversation at the C-level can include how you can help the organization move within the normal range.

In the next chapter, we will begin to accumulate the data collected so that we are able to present our findings to C-level executives. The first step will be to create a financial dashboard. The financial dashboard will be the basis for creating a high-quality business case.

CREATING A FINANCIAL DASHBOARD

A dashboard by definition is a control center that provides output that enables the operator to make informed decisions. It also provides an opportunity to capture key input information that will assist the operator further in making such decisions. In a car or truck, for example, the "low-fuel" light tells drivers that if they don't take action, a problem could occur (running out of gas and being stranded). The action, of course, is to fill the tank with fuel to avoid trouble. A financial dashboard should assimilate the information (results) that you have collected and provide output that will assist your prospects in determining whether your product or service will help them reduce costs, increase revenues, and/or avoid other costs. In addition, this output will provide the necessary tools to understand the effect on their C-Suite metrics. Like the low-fuel light on your car's dashboard, the potential effect on the metrics will be a warning sign of what may happen if your prospects do not take action.

We first need to build the components (both inputs and outputs) of the dashboard. This chapter will explain the basics of creating a comprehensive dashboard that you can use as the basis for your business case.

BUILDING A COMPREHENSIVE FINANCIAL DASHBOARD

At the end of the previous chapter, we had you identify and collect some of the data required to create a financial dashboard. These data are critical to continuing in this chapter. Be sure you have assembled all the components that we discussed, and remember, knowledge is power!

Setup and Preparation

In Chapter 3, we suggested that you use a spreadsheet program to collect the information from your pain-discovery questions. Now is the time to pull together all of the information you collected (e.g., questions, answers, and estimates) into one spreadsheet program. If you recall, we had you create pain-discovery questions to identify pain, and then we had you create questions to capture and calculate current and ongoing cost. We also had you estimate your value. All of this information should be collected in a spreadsheet program and used to populate your dashboard.

Data Rules

The old saying "He who has the data rules!" still holds true today. The problem is that those who have the data don't always know that they have them, and even if they do, they don't necessarily know what to do with them. All too many sales professionals on a pain-discovery call collect information and document it on a legal pad, then either file it in a folder in their desk or enter a shortened version into a sales force automation (SFA) or customer resource management (CRM) system. What good are the data in one of these automated systems or in a desk drawer, if they are not being used for analysis to close a sales opportunity?

The information that you collected throughout the discovery phase of your sales process should be represented in your financial dashboard. At a minimum, you must include your prospect's issues, pains, and goals; current and ongoing cost; and the estimated value that your products and services are capable of delivering. Be sure to offset these entries with an investment breakdown that demonstrates your value to the prospect using some sort of cash flow analysis over a three- to seven-year period. These components are recommended as the minimum you need to include.

To go beyond the minimum output required, we suggest that the data you have collected can be used to help determine the effect that your products and services will have on your prospect's financial reports and key financial metrics, the ones we defined in Chapter 1 as the "C-Suite metrics." They are:

- Return on assets (ROA)

- Return on equity (ROE)

- Earnings

- Operating costs

- Net and gross profit margin

- Payroll as a percentage of sales

- Sales per employee

- Debt-to-equity ratio

- Earnings before interest, taxes, depreciation, and amortization (EBITDA) margin

- Days' sales outstanding (DSO)

You have a distinct advantage over your competition when you use data-gathering tools like pain-discovery questionnaires, total cost of ownership (TCO) models, risk assessments, or value-estimation tools. You will look and become more organized and professional. We believe that there is value in the fact that you are using a consistent data-gathering method, and that the data you have gathered are always available for dissection, interpretation, and analysis.

In addition, the data that you collect throughout the discovery process can be made available and shared with C-level executives. Your data-collection efforts provide you with the information that these same executives are using to set a strategic course of action and to make key buying decisions. The challenge you face is that sometimes your prospects are making buying decisions (or, conversely, nonbuying decisions) based on incomplete, inaccurate, and/or false information. Unless you collect the data, validate them, share your findings, and discuss the C-Suite impact, you are always going to be at the mercy of what your prospects think and feel. The data that you collect and how you present them to your prospect are key parts of a successful sale. As a sales professional, it is your responsibility to assist the buyer in better understanding her issue, pain, or goal; the associated current and ongoing cost; her threshold for pain; and the C-Suite impact; and finally to help her realize that maintaining the status quo is not free. This responsibility comes with great risk and reward.

Risk and Reward

When you go through the process of identifying pain, capturing cost, and calculating future cost, you sometimes end up with nothing. You lose out to a no-decision again. There is always the danger that when your prospects realize the current and future cost, they will prove to be okay with those numbers. Unless you understand and discuss the threshold for pain, you really don't know for sure if you have a buyer. The prospect's personal threshold for pain could be way off in the future.

So you risk spending a tremendous amount of time on an opportunity that may never close. If you have followed this plan from the beginning, you will quickly recognize that we have built in some checks and balances to mitigate this risk. However, it still exists, and it is very real. In later chapters, we will discuss how you can analyze metrics associated with financial reports and determine whether a prospect has the ability to buy from you. There are metrics that reveal a lot more than meets the eye. If you know that a prospect is incapable of purchasing from you or anyone, you can avoid that prospect and save yourself the time, energy, and money spent on chasing him.

Finally, your reward, of course, is the sale itself! If you have discussed the threshold for pain and the impact on the C-Suite metrics with your prospect before now, and the two of you have agreed on obtainable goals for the future, you are in a position to win the sales opportunity. The good news is that if you are discussing your impact on the C-Suite metrics, it won't take years to see your value start to take effect. Your solution should have some short-term impacts on the prospect's financials. Be sure you discuss these impacts and establish financial goals that will take effect over the course of the next 12 to 18 months. That being said, the dashboard is a critical piece in a successful sale to C-level executives.

DASHBOARD COMPONENTS

Keep in mind that the big picture here is to create an interactive financial dashboard that can be used to accomplish the following:

- Consolidate the data collected during discovery in one location.

- Provide the ability to enter assumptions and receive immediate feedback on the impact.

- Establish goals and project the impact that your solution will have on your prospect's issues and pains.

- Display three to seven years of cost/impact data and provide a reality check.

- Capture and display pain and value for side-by-side comparison.

When possible, you must paint a complete picture that can be used by C-level executives to make informed buying decisions. Providing a tool that can be used to capture and display prospects' issues, pains, and goals along with your solution's impact on their financial levers goes a long way toward separating you from the way other companies approach the C-Suite. Putting the competitive advantage aside, your ability to communicate at this level will ensure that you are looked upon as a competent advisor and not just another vendor.

A financial dashboard is the accumulated data that you have collected from your prospect, along with additional calculations to help you project the potential impact from your products and/or services. There are several components that we believe should be included in a financial dashboard, along with some optional areas that may or may not be pertinent to your particular business. We will define the components and outline how to design your financial dashboard so that it will provide your prospects with the data they need to make an informed buying decision.

First, we need a short digression to ensure that you have collected all of the data necessary to populate a financial dashboard. In the previous chapters, we discussed the data necessary to identify pain, capture and calculate costs, estimate values, and measure your value as an impact on a prospect's C-Suite metrics. In Chapter 5, we introduced a new tool that you can use to compare your prospect's C-Suite metrics to industry norms.

Each piece of information you have collected from your prospect using the tools and techniques we have discussed so far should be represented on your financial dashboard. If you skipped a chapter or failed to create the tools necessary to collect the required information, return to that chapter and develop the necessary tool to collect what is needed to complete your financial dashboard.

KEY POINT

A financial dashboard is not the "online" version of the business case; it is the *primary* collection center.

Financial Dashboard Summary Page

The first page of your financial dashboard should be a summary of all of your findings. This summary page is used to provide a synopsis of the findings and results and identify areas that still need input. Here are the suggested sections for the summary page:

- First-year financial summary (investment vs. impact)

- Impact breakdown by financial category

- Financial impact by traditional ROI metrics

- Cash flow summary

- C-Suite metrics summary

- Investment breakdown

- Cost of status quo summary

Each section is designed to provide information on the data that you collected during the pain-discovery phase of the sales process. We have added some areas where you can apply the data you have collected and calculate the estimated impacts that your products and services may have on your prospect's financial levers.

We will discuss each of these sections and provide spreadsheet examples that you can use to design your own dashboard. *Note:* We strongly suggest that you automate your financial dashboard using a tool like Microsoft Excel.

Figure 6-1 shows an example of a dashboard summary page. This summary is often used to spawn a discussion on issues, pains, and goals and your financial impact as it relates to your prospect's financial levers.

FIGURE 6-1

ABC Enterprises   January 2, 2009

This dashboard is used to consolidate data and provide the baseline information needed to create a compelling business case. The analysis below consists of financial summary information, investment information, and status quo costs. As with any dashboard, we require input and provide informative output that you can use to assess your current situation and estimate the value we are capable of delivering.

First-Year Financial Summary *(Risk Adjusted)*	
First-Year Investment:	$900,000
First-Year Impact:	($643,000)

First-Year Category Summary *(Risk Adjusted)*	
Impact from Cost Reductions:	$225,000
Impact from Revenue Increases:	$82,700
External Savings Estimated:	$57,300

Project Financial Summary *(Risk Adjusted)*	
Total Investment:	$1,638,000
Total Impact: *(Risk Adjusted)*	$2,594,000
Return on Investment:	158%
Payback Period: *(Months)*	22.7
Net Present Value:	$737,620
Internal Rate of Return:	48%

Cash Flow Summary	
Number of years included:	3 years
Investment:	$1,638,000
Return: *(Risk Adjusted)*	$2,594,000
Cumulative Return:	$956,000

C-Suite Summary		
C-Suite Category	Current	Revised
Net Profit Margin:	$2,400,000	$2,582,439
Operating Costs:	$11,000,000	$10,858,704
Sales / Employee:	$3,000,000	$3,228,049
Payroll as Percentage of Sales:	25.0%	22.9%
Earnings:	$2,400,000	$2,407,119

Investment Summary	
Hardware	$500,000
Software	$460,000
Consulting	$100,000
Maintenance	$200,000
Internal costs	$225,000
Upgrades	$90,000
Materials	$45,000
Miscellaneous	$3,000
Other	$15,000

Status Quo Summary	
Three-year cost of status quo:	$6,750,000
Daily cost of status quo:	$8,654
Revised daily cost of status quo:	$4,308
Decision delay cost:	$134,769

First-Year Financial Summary

This section is used to inform the buyer of the first-year cost of your product or service and the estimated impact. It is not unusual for the first-year cost to exceed the impact, resulting in a negative impact figure on your summary page. This says that your return on investment is longer than one year.

The detailed data that feed this section come from two areas of your financial dashboard. You can see in the example in Figure 6-1 that there is an investment section that collects the expected investment over a specific period of time. In our example, the investment covers a period of three years. The first-year investment is drawn from this section.

The first-year impact, however, is drawn from the responses to your discovery questions. We like to display the first-year results in columns that can be used to summarize your prospect's responses. We break the details down by cost reductions, revenue increases, and cost avoidances (pain categories). (See Figure 6-2 for a breakdown of cost reductions.)

FIGURE 6-2

Cost Reductions	Current Cost	Revised Cost	Value Delivered
Annual FTE cost reduction from reducing number of days less productive new hires remain on staff:	$173,077	$69,231	$103,846
Annual start-up and recruiting cost reduction:	$53,500	$16,050	$37,450
Cost reduction from reducing number of days to close a sale:	$6,300,000	$4,325,000	$1,975,000
Summary total of value delivered:	$6,526,577	$4,410,281	$2,116,296

Pain Categories

This section of your financial dashboard includes a breakdown by pain categories: cost reductions, revenue increases, and cost avoidances. The value inventory that you created in Chapter 2 breaks down your value proposition into one or more of these categories. This section is designed to allow you to hold a high-level conversation with your prospect on where the most impact is going to come from by financial category. This discussion involves the strategic direction and priorities of the organization. There may be major initiatives on cost reductions, or perhaps a focus on increasing revenues. Another priority could be to avoid hiring additional personnel—making cost avoidance a high priority. The category breakdown can be displayed for the entire project (three to seven years), by year of the analysis, or for only the first year.

Project Financial Summary: Traditional ROI Metrics

In the project financial summary section, we display several calculations, beginning with total investment and total impact. Total investment will be carried over from the investment section of the dashboard (more on this later). Total impact, however, comes from the work you did in earlier chapters when you captured current cost and extrapolated that cost over a three- to seven-year period. The three- to seven-year breakdown is summarized and then totaled for the dashboard. The format for the detail is really up to you. We like to break it down by cost reductions, revenue increases, and cost avoidances. Figure 6-3 is an example of how we display a three-year analysis.

FIGURE 6-3

Cost Reductions		Current Year	Year Two	Year Three
Annual FTE cost reduction from reducing number of days less productive new hires remain on staff:	Current Cost:	$173,077	$272,596	$445,240
	Value Delivered:	$103,846	$179,913	$323,245
Annual start-up and recruiting cost reduction:	Current Cost:	$53,500	$56,175	$58,984
	Value Delivered:	$37,450	$43,255	$49,959
Calculated annual revenue increase due to increased revenue per marketing dollar spent on leads:	Current Cost:	$353,000	$412,000	$501,000
	Value Delivered:	$125,000	$178,000	$291,000
Total cost reduction savings over three-year period:		$266,296	$401,168	$664,204

We like to display some of the traditional ROI calculations in this section, too. Return on investment is a simple calculation in which you divide the total investment (all years included) by the projected total impact of your solution (all years included). If you fail to return and measure your actual impact, the ROI percentage is just a number. If you treat this number as a goal, and return annually (at a minimum) to measure your success, then the ROI percentage takes on a whole new meaning. It becomes a real metric to be measured on a regular basis.

Payback period is another figure that is often used to project the success of a project. The calculation for payback period is total investment divided by total impact, multiplied by the number of months of analysis. For example, if the investment over a three-year period is $1,638,000, the projected return or impact is $2,594,000, and the analysis is over a three-year period, the calculation would be as follows:

($1,638,000 ÷ $2,594,000) × 36 (months) = 22.7 months payback

Payback period should not start until the project is running at full speed. Be sure to add start-up time to the payback period to make it more accurate.

C-Suite executives will sometimes use the projected payback period to determine the viability of taking on a project. If it takes too long to reach payback, a project is likely to get sidelined before it ever begins.

There are two additional calculations that are often found in financial-based sales tools. They are net present value (NPV) and internal rate of return (IRR). Our experience has been that most financial people will do their own math on these figures. However, there is no harm in including them in your financial dashboard.

Let's begin with a simple definition of net present value: the difference between the present value of cash inflows and the present value of cash outflows. NPV is typically used in capital budgeting to analyze the profitability of a long-term investment or project.

To calculate NPV, we like to use the Microsoft Excel function. It is very simple to build a table with the variable required by Excel. (See Figure 6-4.)

FIGURE 6-4

	Initial Investment	Year 1	Year 2	Year 3
Investment	($490,000)	($518,000)	($305,000)	($325,000)
Return	$0	$365,000	$975,000	$1,254,000
Net return	($490,000)	($153,000)	$670,000	$929,000
Discount rate	5.0%			
NPV		($605,442)	($26,671)	$737,620

The investment line is taken from the dashboard and multiplied by −1 to create a cost line. The return line is captured from the dashboard summary lines of impact by year. The net is a simple calculation of subtracting the investment from the impact. The discount rate is the rate at which you can borrow from a bank.

NPV is a standard Excel function, like "Sum." So if you are using Microsoft Excel (again, our recommendation), the way you type the formula into the spreadsheet is displayed. The NPV formula = NPV (discount rate, value 1, value 2, . . . , value n). In our example, there would be three values representing the summary of initial net through Year 3 net. Refer to Excel "help" if you need additional information.

Internal rate of return is essentially the rate of growth that a project is expected to generate. Generally speaking, the higher a project's IRR, the more desirable it is to undertake the project. We use the same table to calculate IRR. (See Figure 6-5.)

Using all of the same numbers that we used in our explanation for NPV, you can see that IRR is calculated as a percentage. IRR is also a standard Excel function. The Excel formula for IRR is (sum of initial net through third year net × discount rate). Once again, be sure to refer to Excel "help" for more information on the format of the formula.

FIGURE 6-5

	Initial Investment	Year 1	Year 2	Year 3
Investment	($490,000)	($518,000)	($305,000)	($325,000)
Return	$0	$365,000	$975,000	$1,254,000
Net return	($490,000)	($153,000)	$670,000	$929,000
Discount rate	5.0%			
IRR		N/A	2%	48%
NPV		($605,442)	($26,671)	$737,620

Cash Flow

The next section of your dashboard should include some sort of cash flow analysis. We provide a summary of three- to seven-year cash flows that includes year-by-year investment, projected impact, and cumulative return. Figure 6-6 shows a sample of the detail that we provide in the body of the financial dashboard.

FIGURE 6-6

Cash Flow Analysis

	Year 1	Year 2	Year 3	Summary Total
Investment:	$1,008,000	$305,000	$325,000	$1,638,000
Return:	$365,000	$975,000	$1,254,000	$2,594,000
Net return:	($643,000)	$670,000	$929,000	$956,000
Cumulative return:	($643,000)	$27,000	$956,000	$956,000

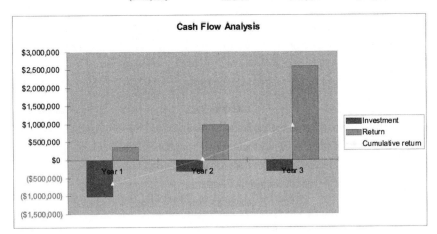

Note that the first-year investment includes our initial investment plus all Year 1 cash layouts.

In Figure 6-6, we created a simple cash flow analysis for a three-year period. It is not unusual to stretch out cash flow for five or even seven years. There are two critical components of this display: net return and cumulative return. Net return displays each year's cost against the value expected to be returned in that year. The obvious impact on the C-Suite is cash flow each year. However, this is not the only picture being displayed here. The cumulative return displays the impact of the accumulated cash position year by year as it progresses through the three to seven years. As you can see from the chart, in the first year, you are in a negative state; there is a $643,000 loss. In Year 2, however, you more than make up the loss and display the cumulative return of $27,000. The nice thing about this display is that you are able to see the progress that the project is making each year. The line running through the chart displays the cumulative return. As you can clearly see, it is not until Year 2 that the company finally begins to see a positive cash flow.

Together, the chart and the graph tell a story of how the prospect's investment will affect key financial levers like cash flow, net profit, return on assets, debt-to-equity ratio, payback period, and potential return on investment.

One last note: An excellent feature of Microsoft Excel is the fact that your charts are dynamic. What this means is that as you make changes in components like investment amounts or returns on your dashboard, the chart will adjust automatically. This enables you to play "what if" games with the information. For example, you can adjust the investment and see the payback period and cash flow shift either up or down. Remember, the dashboard needs to be able to accept input if it is to provide useful output as it relates to the cost of the status quo and the C-Suite metrics.

C-Suite Summary

The C-Suite effect should be a key component of the financial dashboard. In fact, this is where we suggest you create the baseline input for comparison. On the summary page of the financial dashboard, we display only some of the metrics in their current state and the estimated revised state after we have delivered our value. The detail breakdown needs to be included so that you are able to input the information required to gain a better understanding of the status quo. (See Figure 6-7.)

FIGURE 6-7

C-Suite Summary		
C-Suite Category	**Current**	**Revised**
Net profit margin	$2,400,000	$2,491,603
Operating costs	$11,000,000	$10,858,704
Sales / employee	$3,000,000	$3,493,449
Payroll as percentage of sales	25.0%	24.5%
Earnings	$24,000	$2,406,869

By displaying the summary on the first page, you are establishing the groundwork for a conversation at the C-level. Most executives will look at your first page and want to discuss in detail the data that they don't understand, object to, or don't believe. Discussions of C-Suite metrics could fall into any of these categories. To be able to summarize the C-Suite metrics results, you must be able to first accumulate the impact, enter the status quo, and calculate the results.

We will begin with how you collect the information to establish the status quo. When you created your value inventory, we had you add an additional column that included the C-Suite metrics. You will want to refer to this document when you create a background table in your financial dashboard. (See Figure 6-8.)

This table contains 11 summary calculations that we made when we were estimating our value to the prospect. Each line on the table represents a primary discovery question and the impact results. We capture the impact in Column 1, followed by the impact on each C-Suite metric in the other columns. Notice that most of the impacts affect multiple columns. The summary totals at the bottom of the table (Figure 6-9) will become the default impacts for the financial dashboard.

FIGURE 6-8

C-Suite Accumulations	Value	ROA	ROE	Earnings	Operating Cost	Net Profit	Gross Profit	Payroll / % Sales	Sales / Employee	EBITA	Profit Margin
Security											
Security Breach - cost avoidance	$51,961	$51,961	$51,961	$51,961	$51,961	$51,961				$51,961	$51,961
Internal Call Center											
Labor cost / higher 1st call	$81,600	$81,600	$81,600	$81,600	$81,600	$81,600		$81,600		$81,600	$81,600
Labor cost / Call time resolution:	$408,000	$408,000	$408,000	$408,000	$408,000	$408,000		$408,000		$408,000	$408,000
Labor cost / multi-task	$250,500	$250,500	$250,500	$250,500	$250,500	$250,500		$250,500		$250,500	$250,500
Labor cost / truck roll savings:	$543,500	$543,500	$543,500	$543,500	$543,500	$543,500		$543,500		$543,500	$543,500

FIGURE 6-9

One Year Impact - **Financial Statement Metric Analysis**			
Metric Analyzed	**Current**	**Revised**	**Change**
Net Profit Margin	8%		6.7%
Pretax profit:	$2,400,000	$2,571,135	
Annual revenue:	$30,000,000		
Operating Costs	$21,254,000	$19,250,000	-9.4%
Percent of total revenue:	70.85%	64.17%	
Earnings			
Revenue:	$30,000,000		
Operating expense:	21,254,000		
Taxes:	$6,165,000		
Earnings	$2,581,000	$2,407,088	0.3%
Payroll as Percent of Sales			
Annual Payroll:	$11,875,000	$11,625,675	
Revenue:	$30,000,000		
Percentage:	39.6%	38.8%	-2.1%
Sales / Employee			
Revenue:	$30,000,000	$32,139,191	
Number of employees:	125		
Current sales / employee:	$240,000	$257,114	6.7%

C-Suite Details

We realize that this is the first time you are seeing this information laid out in this format. It can be a bit overwhelming, so let's break it down into smaller pieces that make it much easier to understand. First, notice the requirement for input on several of the metric calculations. If you know the answers to the input required from your research, enter them before sharing this page with your prospect. Then validate or confirm your entries before moving on.

In the example discussed here, you have chosen five of the C-Suite metrics to display. The reason for this is that the value you deliver affects only these five metrics. Some of our clients use eight or nine of the metrics, and some use only a couple. It doesn't matter how many of the metrics you use on your dashboard as long as they are pertinent to the value that you are capable of delivering.

Now, return to your value inventory and select the metrics that have the most impact on your prospect's financial reports. Almost everyone uses net profit margin, earnings, and operating cost. Figure 6-10 shows net profit margin.

Early in the sales process, we asked the question, "What is your annual revenue?" We then entered (or defaulted) the answer into the dashboard. Any time you are able to default data into the dashboard, doing so is to your advantage because there will not be any additional discussion on the validity of the data. All you need to ask is for your prospect to "confirm" that the data are correct. Do your research (see Chapter 4), and gather as much information as you can.

FIGURE 6-10

Financial Statement Metric Analysis			
Metric Analyzed	**Current**	**Revised**	**Change**
Net Profit Margin	$2,400,000	$2,571,135	6.7%
Pretax Profit	8.0%		
Revenue:	$30,000,000		

Since we had the revenue figure, we just needed to ask for a pretax profit percentage, and then we automatically calculated the company's current net profit margin of $2,400,000. If the prospect is a publicly held company, these figures (net profit margin and revenue) are available in its annual report or through investor relations.

The "Revised" column displays the financial impact that your estimated values will have on the company's net profit margin. The revised revenue is now $32,139,191. All you have to do is multiply this figure by the 8 percent net profit and you will see the revised net profit (Column 2). This is your solution's total impact on net profit. Remember, net profit is affected by both cost reductions and revenue increases, so you must include both when calculating impact. (See Figure 6-11.)

FIGURE 6-11

C-Suite Accumulations	Value	Net Profit	Op. Cost	Sales/Emp
Calculated additional revenue recaptured from increased pipeline:	$150,000	$150,000		$150,000
Calculated additional revenue recaptured from increase close ratio (less closed pipeline):	$982,000	$982,000		$982,000
Calculated annual revenue increase due to increased number of appointments:	$0	$0		$0
Calculated annual revenue gained due to increase in cross selling:	$424,800	$424,800		$424,800
Calculated annual revenue gained due to increase in up-selling:	$178,416	$178,416		$178,416
Annual FTE cost reduction from reducing number of days less productive new hires remain on staff	$103,846	-$103,846	$103,846	$103,846
Annual start-up and recruiting cost reduction:	$37,450	-$37,450	$37,450	
Calculated annual revenue recaptured from a reduction in discounting:	$351,220	$351,220		$351,220
Cost reduction in reducing number of days to close a sale:	$0		$0	
Calculated annual revenue increase due to increased revenue per marketing dollar spent on leads:	$96,755	$96,755		$96,755
Calculated increase in revenue due to shorter start-up period for new hires:	$97,297	$97,297		$97,297
	$2,421,784	$2,139,192	$141,296	$2,384,334

Here is one more example of how to use your table to calculate the change in the C-Suite metrics.

Each of the C-Suite metrics and its calculation should be displayed on the screen with the original or current status and the estimated revised status based on the projected impact of your solution.

Another common value delivered in a business-to-business (B2B) sale is a reduction in overhead or operating costs. We add the metric "percentage of total revenue" to give the change a little more boost in value to the prospect. (See Figure 6-12.)

FIGURE 6-12

Financial Statement Metric Analysis			
Operating Costs	$21,254,000	$19,250,000	-9.4%
Percentage of total revenue:	70.85%	64.17%	

As you can see from the example in Figure 6-12, the annual operating costs are projected to be reduced by $2,004,000. The 9.43 percent reduction would be reflected in the table that we use to track the impact on all of the C-Suite metrics.

The financial dashboard summary page can include current vs. revised, or you can get more elaborate and break out the elements of each metric and create a simple graph of the results.

There are two metrics that we use to monitor an organization's most expensive asset: human capital. The first is "payroll as a percentage of sales," and the second is "sales per employee."

There are two components that make up payroll as a percentage of sales. (See Figure 6-13.)

FIGURE 6-13

Financial Statement Metric Analysis			
Payroll as Percentage of Sales			
Annual Payroll:	$11,875,000	$11,625,675	2.1%
Revenue:	$30,000,000		
Percentage:	39.6%	38.8%	

The first component is a movement in revenue. If your solution affects revenue in a positive or negative way, then the payroll as a percentage of sales will be affected. For example, if you are able to increase a customer's revenue without affecting its labor cost, you will lower its payroll as a percentage of sales. If you are able to reduce the company's labor cost with no effect on revenue, the same result will occur; you will lower payroll as a percentage of revenue. In our example in Figure 6-13, we do both: We lower payroll by $103,846, and we increase revenue by $2,280,487. The net effect is a reduction of 2.1 percent in payroll as a percentage of sales.

Sales per employee is a metric that we often use to get an understanding of an organization's size. (See Figure 6-14.)

FIGURE 6-14

Financial Statement Metric Analysis			
Sales / Employee			
Revenue:	$30,000,000	$32,139,191	
Number of Employees:	125		
Current Sales / Employee:	$240,000	$257,114	6.7%

By increasing revenue and keeping the number of employees steady, you increase the average sales per employee. The same is true if you help reduce the number of staff members and keep the revenue steady.

Rather than discussing ROI and net present value, you are now capable of discussing your solution and its impact on net profit, operating costs, sales per employee, payroll as a percentage of sales, and earnings. These are all key metrics that a C-level executive is interested in moving. Remember that there are more than a dozen metrics available to use in this exercise.

Investment

You will want to include an investment section in your dashboard. It is critical that you capture three to seven years of costs when developing your financial dashboard. The investment spread over the years is used for status quo calculations (shown in the next section), ROI, NPV, and IRR. We like to include a small chart on the summary page that shows how the investment declines over the life of the project. (See Figure 6-15.)

Status Quo

We talk a lot about how crucial it is for sales professionals to help their prospects understand that maintaining the status quo is not always free, and that for every day they choose to *not make* a decision, there is a cost. Think of it in terms of a broken bone: If it goes untreated, the pain will continue. Eventually it may "heal itself," but there are repercussions if you

FIGURE 6-15

Investment Category	Deposit	Year 1	Year 2	Year 3	Summary Totals
Hardware	$125,000	$125,000	$125,000	$125,000	$500,000
Software	$175,000	$175,000	$50,000	$60,000	$460,000
Consulting		$100,000			$100,000
Maintenance	$50,000	$50,000	$50,000	$50,000	$200,000
Internal costs		$65,000	$75,000	$85,000	$225,000
Upgrades	$90,000				$90,000
Materials	$45,000				$45,000
Miscellaneous		$3,000			$3,000
Other	$5,000		$5,000	$5,000	$15,000
Summary Totals	$490,000	$518,000	$305,000	$325,000	

Total Investment: $1,638,000

Annualized Investment: $546,000

don't take care of it, such as arthritis, phantom pain, possible infection, and so on. This is the same thing that happens with corporate pain. By identifying the issue or pain and capturing the current and ongoing cost of that pain, you can show your prospect that if the pain goes untreated, there will be repercussions in terms of the effect on the C-Suite metrics, financial reports, shareholder value, and the overall health of the organization. The effect will lead to many bad things that businesses may have to go through, such as layoffs, budget cuts, or perhaps even bankruptcy. Figure 6-16 gives an example of how you can graphically display the point that the status quo and decision delay are not free.

Let's break this example down into separate components. The first component is the current cost of the status quo. We believe this is the most important number in this section because it speaks right to the threshold for pain. This number is the accumulation of all the "costs" you have gathered from your prospect through the course of the pain-discovery questioning. In the previous section, we already captured this information by category. All you need to do is add up the total of all the costs over the three-year period and enter the number here.

Next, calculate the current daily cost of the status quo (calculation: current cost divided by number of years, then divided by number of working days in a year). The reason we use a daily cost calculation is that short-term pain (daily) is easier to identify with (feel) and is typically more painful to the buyer. If a prospect realizes that its pain is costing more than $8,000 a day, it will *seem* more painful than $6 million over three years.

FIGURE 6-16

Cost Reductions: Status Quo "Cost" Calculation Summary		
**Financial Analysis**		_**Daily**_
Current cost of status quo:	$6,750,000	$8,654
Revised cost of status quo:	$3,360,000	$4,308
Value delivered / per day:	$3,390,000	$4,346
Investment per day:	$1,638,000	$2,100
Enter number of days for decision delay:		60
Calculated decision delay cost:		$134,769

Status Quo Analysis

	Year 1	Year 2	Year 3
■ Cost Status Quo	1500000	2350000	2900000
☐ Revised Cost Status quo	700000	950000	1710000

Beneath the current cost is the revised cost information. This calculation is done by simply subtracting the value that you expect to deliver from the current cost and repeating the previous daily cost calculations. Once again, if you broke out cost and value by category, you already have the figures. All you will need to do is add them up and enter them in the template.

Now that you have laid out the current and ongoing cost and potential value side of the equation, it is necessary for you to add the prospect's investment side of the value equation. As a vendor, you will, of course, charge to deliver this value, so it is necessary to include the cost or investment per day (calculation: total investment divided by the same number of years and the same number of working days in a year). We broke down the current cost and estimated the value and revised cost on a daily basis; now we will need to break down the investment on a daily basis, too.

You can quickly look at this picture and say, "Would you spend $2,100 per day to get back $4,346 per day in value?" Who wouldn't? (See Figure 6-17.)

FIGURE 6-17

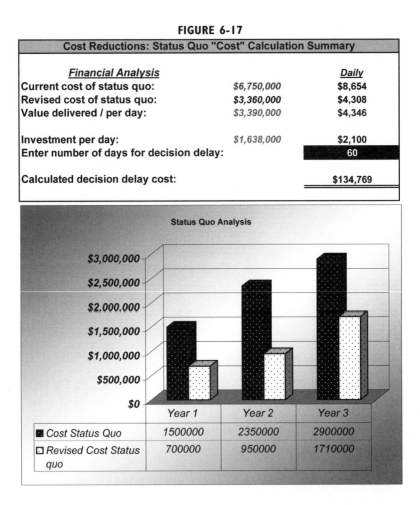

Cost Reductions: Status Quo "Cost" Calculation Summary		
Financial Analysis		*Daily*
Current cost of status quo:	$6,750,000	$8,654
Revised cost of status quo:	$3,360,000	$4,308
Value delivered / per day:	$3,390,000	$4,346
Investment per day:	$1,638,000	$2,100
Enter number of days for decision delay:		60
Calculated decision delay cost:		$134,769

Status Quo Analysis

	Year 1	Year 2	Year 3
■ Cost Status Quo	1500000	2350000	2900000
□ Revised Cost Status quo	700000	950000	1710000

To carry this point a little further, when you subtract the cost per day from the value per day, it becomes the "daily cost of decision delay." What this means is that for every day the prospect delays making a decision, it is losing the difference between cost and value per day delivered. In the example in Figure 6-17, it is $2,246 lost for each day it takes to make a decision. If you input the estimated number of days that a decision will take, your screen should calculate the cost of decision delay. In this example, a 60-day decision cycle is going to cost the prospect $134,769. This is powerful information to have and share with your prospect!

Detail Analysis

The final section of your financial dashboard that we want to discuss should include summaries of questions that you asked in your pain-discovery exercise. Repeating and displaying this information grouped by cost reductions, revenue increases, and cost avoidances will enable you to better understand the value areas that are most affected by your solution. In addition, it is a confirmation that you discussed the issue, captured the prospect's cost, and estimated the potential value that you are capable of delivering. (See Figure 6-18.)

FIGURE 6-18

Cost Reductions	Current Cost	Revised Cost	Value Delivered
Annual FTE cost reducing less productive staff sooner:	$173,077	$69,231	$103,846
Annual start up and recruiting cost reduction:	$53,500	$16,050	$37,450
Cost reduction from reducing number of days to close a sale:	$3,360,000	$2,653,140	$706,860
Summary total of value delivered:	$3,586,577	$2,738,421	$848,156

The example in Figure 6-18 is the cost reduction section of a dashboard that we designed for one of our customers that specializes in training new hires to be more productive more quickly. There are three impacts identified in the figure: (1) the cost of keeping a "bad" hire on your payroll too long, (2) the expense of recruiting, and (3) the amount of time (cost) a new hire spends being unproductive before closing his first sale. Notice that we listed the current cost of the status quo in the first column. Establishing the current situation (cost) is always your starting point, before estimating value and discussing threshold. This is also a reminder that your prospect has a current cost that is not going to go away. In the last column, we list the value or goal. Finally, in the middle column, we simply subtract the value from the current cost and display a revised cost.

It is important to provide both Year 1 estimates and the three- to seven-year estimates and analysis. You are laying the groundwork for numerous discussions on short-term value and long-term value as they relate to your prospect's pain level.

We assume that you are using the sales tools shown in this book throughout your sales process to gather prospect information. Now it is necessary to pull all of your findings into one central location to be used for building your business case and proposal. Do not be confused and think that a financial dashboard is a business case. A financial dashboard is the primary source for the data required to produce your business case. You will want to customize this document to fit your industry.

SUMMARY

The financial dashboard is a critical part of your sales tool arsenal. Accumulating and displaying the information you have discovered in a readable, simple-to-interpret manner is a major advantage for you during the sales process. Too often, we see a spreadsheet full of numbers and semi-populated graphs on dashboards that our customers have attempted to put together. These attempts only make you look amateurish and nonprofessional.

Be sure to include sections that cover:

- Issues, pains, and goals that have been identified and the costs and values associated with each

- Goals established for reducing costs, increasing revenue, and avoiding other costs

- Cash flow analysis over a three- to seven-year period

- Investment breakdown for three to seven years

- Cost of status quo and decision delay calculations

- C-Suite metrics and your value impact

The financial dashboard should give you the opportunity to make changes and play "what if" games with the data. In addition, the dashboard will help you with your discussion on the threshold for pain and establish the areas in which you offer the greatest value. Finally, a dashboard that includes the C-Suite effect will drive a conversation at different levels within any prospect's organization. You must be able to sit down and discuss each section of your dashboard prior to producing a business case analysis.

There are many other components that we did not cover that you may want to add to your dashboard. You may wish to include additional financial metrics, industry comparisons for the C-Suite, case study results, or even more graphics. Remember to create an environment in which the data you collect can be interpreted and applied to the impact on the C-Suite metrics.

> **KEY POINT**
> Always include on your dashboard any discovery information that will potentially move a financial lever (C-Suite metric).

As a sales professional, you are responsible for gathering the data used in the dashboard. Use the many tools in the market, including Jigsaw, InsideView, or Hoovers. Use your own CFO to gain confidence in your C-Suite metric calculations and discussions. And finally, always include a conversation on the status quo. Remember, "The status quo is not free!"

PRESENTING YOUR C-SUITE FINDINGS

The presentation of the material you have collected can sometimes be overwhelming to a prospect. In this chapter, we will cover the use of presentation options, formatting, graphics usage, and content. Each section will help you lay out the best design for you (and others in your organization) to use to present the material in a manner that is creative, concise, and complete.

Presenting the findings of your research is not always easy. We have reviewed ROI models, PowerPoint™ presentations, proposals, and many other ways of delivering information that sales professionals have created for their prospects, and it is a sorry state of affairs. Sometimes the value gets lost in the presentation because it is too difficult to understand the material that is being presented. Many salespeople seem to want to overwhelm their prospects with their knowledge and tend to spew out a lot of irrelevant material at inopportune times. Our advice to you is to keep it simple and keep it relevant.

Over the years, we have examined hundreds of presentations from big companies, small organizations, and many boutiques in between, and we believe that the effectiveness of your presentation boils down to these eight very important topics:

1. Objectivity of interpretation

2. Credibility of the data collected

3. Accuracy

4. Graphics

5. Educational content

6. Both value and costs presented

7. Creative output

8. C-Suite effect

We believe that some of these criteria are more critical than others; however, each of them is equally dependent upon the success of the others. We will briefly dissect each of these topics and give you tips and ideas on what to aim for in the presentation, as well as how best to use your sales presentation.

OBJECTIVITY OF INTERPRETATION

Objectivity is defined by the *American Heritage Dictionary* as "[being] uninfluenced by emotions or personal prejudices." When a sales professional calls on a prospect, a certain lack of objectivity in her approach is expected. You are (and should be) biased toward the products and services that you are selling. To offset that personal bias, it is important that the sales tools you use throughout your process are unbiased and objective. As you gather information from your prospects, they expect that your presentation will be biased toward your organization. And, let's face it, most of the time it is.

After all, you spent hours, days, or perhaps weeks working through the discovery process. You probably worked on a demonstration to prove your value. You took the time and effort to develop a comprehensive proposal and ROI presentation. The reason that your output or presentation of value is not entirely believable to prospects is that you developed it. Simply put, *you* are the problem.

How do you make your presentation more objective? This will not be easy if you insist on inserting your "opinions," "beliefs," and "values" into the data-collection process and ultimately into the presentation process. Let's go back to the point right after you've built your value inventory, when you first develop your discovery questions. The questions you ask to gather the data you need to complete an objective business case must themselves be credible and objective. They should not show bias. For example, which of the following scenarios is a better way to extract information from your prospect?

Scenario 1: "Ms. Prospect, I know you are paying taxes on ghost or overvalued assets. Am I right?"

Scenario 2: "Ms. Prospect, some of our customers are paying taxes on ghost or overvalued assets. Do you think you are, too? How do you feel about that? Please tell me more."

Notice that in Scenario 1, your opinion or "knowledge" dominated the questioning: "I know you are paying taxes . . ." What *you* know or *think* you know is irrelevant. In Scenario 2, however, you ask the question using social proof from "some" of your other customers, and you ask how the prospect feels. The follow-up encourages your prospect to "tell me more." Obviously, Scenario 2 is the better way to approach and discuss the issue of paying taxes on ghost or overvalued assets with the prospect. What you think at this point—even when you know it is true—is only going to get in the way of your sales process. Using a concept that includes experience from other customers (what we refer to as "social proof") is always more acceptable when discussing issues that your prospects may be facing.

Here is a litmus test to get a better understanding of whether you have created pain-discovery questions that are objective. Ask yourself each of these questions and review your answer against our analysis that follows:

- Did I create this questionnaire based on the *features and benefits* that I see in my product?

- Did I consider the issues and pains in the *industries we sell into*, and develop my value proposition accordingly?

- Did I educate my prospect on *the market pains*, as well as the potential value he can receive when using my products?

If your answer to the first question ("Did I create this questionnaire based on the features and benefits that I see in my product?") is yes, then you do not have the objectivity required to understand the marketplace's issues. You clearly were influenced by your emotions and your personal prejudices toward your own products and services. (See the *American Heritage Dictionary* definition of objectivity given earlier.)

Obviously, you understand your product's features. You now must understand the issues that you can resolve with those features. (Refer to your value inventory document.) First ask yourself, "Does my stated feature address the issues that I have captured in my marketplace?" If you approach prospects by pushing your features and benefits, while ignoring their need for a solution to a specific problem, you will be judged as just another vendor. Developing your value inventory and using it to create objective discovery questions will provide you with a unique approach and insight into industry issues and pains. This is a major advantage when you are presenting your solution to your prospect. You have insight into all the reasons that people buy from you, their business issue, and their desired outcome. You also know the link between the stakeholder and the problem, and, finally, you know your value as it relates to the prospect's problem and the C-Suite metrics. This knowledge is invaluable throughout the sales process, but especially during your presentation to project more objectivity on your part.

Your answer to the second question ("Did I consider the issues and pains in the industries we sell into, and develop my value proposition accordingly?") must be a resounding *yes!* Why does it matter if you consider the market's issues and pains when presenting your recommendations? Because your value is of value to your prospects only if it resolves a problem that they currently have and that they acknowledge they have. How many times have you met sales professionals who are so excited about their product that they start spouting off the features and benefits before you ever get an opportunity to point out how much you don't care? It goes something like this:

SALES PROFESSIONAL: "Good afternoon, how are you?"

YOU: "Fine, thank you. I am considering buying a riding lawn mower."

SALES PROFESSIONAL: "Great; we sell many brands. The most reliable is Simplicity, but we carry Toro and Snapper too."

YOU: "Well, I am less concerned about the lawn mower aspect than the leaf gatherer and the snowplow."

SALES PROFESSIONAL: "I see. Well, the Simplicity comes with all sorts of attachments, and will last you 20 years. It has a 46-inch cutting deck, Kohler 23-horsepower engine, and, look, you can see how much gas is in it, too."

YOU: "Reliability is nice, but I look at this as a five- to eight-year investment. I really just don't want to rake leaves again, and I hate shoveling snow."

SALES PROFESSIONAL: "You don't care about quality?"

YOU: "Yes, I care about quality, but I don't care to keep something for 20 years. I just want something to pick up leaves and plow snow."

You can see that this conversation is going nowhere. The sales professional never really acknowledges what you wanted most in a riding lawn mower. You said several times that gathering leaves and plowing snow are the most important considerations to you. The point here is to ask the questions that drive the value. Get a better understanding of *what your prospect wants or needs,* and don't ever assume that she knows what you are talking about. In our example, the salesperson spouted off about engines and cutting decks, and the prospect really didn't care: "I just want something to pick up leaves and plow snow."

Your presentation must inspire a feeling or paint a picture that your prospects can project themselves into. Last year, I sat through a time-share presentation. Time-share sales professionals sell dreams. They first ask, "Is there anywhere in the world you want to visit?" Next, they tell you that you can visit anywhere in the entire world through their "time-share trade" program. Suddenly, you are thinking about all of the places you want to go. They help you "feel" the benefits of purchasing a time-share. They ask you what you want to do on vacation or what you are looking for in a room or a location. They sell sun, snow, oceans, and mountains. They are helping you dream about what you want to be doing the next time you are on vacation. You almost sell yourself. I had to stop and step back before I had talked myself into buying a time-share.

We always tell our sales force to have the pain discussion and help the prospect "feel" the pain. Your discovery discussion and presentation should make your prospects genuinely worry about what will happen in the future if they don't do something about the problem they have today.

Using your value inventory as a foundation for the presentation, you are able to correlate industry pain to your value proposition. This, in turn, will help you become more objective in your presentation.

Our third question ("Did I educate my prospect on the market pains, as well as the potential value he can receive when using my products?") must be answered yes, too. When you get the opportunity to ask questions of your prospect, you need to ensure that this is an educational process for both of you. Keep in mind early in the process how important your solution is to the prospect. (See Figure 7-1.)

Your questions need to uncover pain, drive value, and, at the same time, inform the prospect of issues that you expect to resolve. This is a give-and-take performance. For example, when Rockwell Automation sales professionals are working with prospects to buy a process-control maintenance system, they may ask questions like:

- How much downtime do you experience after normal business hours? (This question has indirectly informed the prospect of your after-hours support and drives the conversation in the direction that you want.)

FIGURE 7-1

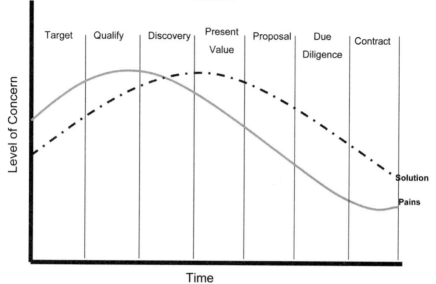

Target | Qualify | Discovery | Present Value | Proposal | Due Diligence | Contract

Level of Concern

Time

Solution
Pains

* Do you have the ability to download product fixes? (Once again, you are asking a question that implies that you have the capability of allowing end users to download update programs and fixes.)

A well-thought-out set of discovery questions will help you gain your prospects' confidence, provide you with the information you need to assess their problems, and, of course, educate your prospects on some of the value that you bring to the table. In addition, you are likely to uncover pain that they didn't realize they were experiencing. Your presentation of the discovery material and recommendations should objectively lay out the issues, pains, and goals discussed (and agreed upon); the value that your products and services deliver; the investment required; and the C-Suite impact, and should provide a recommendation for strategic deployment.

Lack of objectivity is one of the primary reasons that presentations fail. The data you collected should be presented without opinion. Your findings and conclusions must be objective, credible, and backed up by fact.

Social proof, such as stating what your "typical" customer has experienced or giving an example of a specific customer, is always helpful. Use research firms like Gartner Group, Forrester Research, or Aberdeen to back up your claims and potential impact on the C-Suite metrics. These firms perform studies on all sorts of topics. Look for information relating to your industry on their web site and purchase the right to quote or cite their research.

Objectivity is one of the most important aspects of your presentation. It will overlap with the next topic: credibility.

CREDIBILITY OF THE DATA COLLECTED

When discussing credibility, you face issues similar to those you face with objectivity. Ask yourself, "Is my presentation credible?" Would you personally believe the sales points and recommendations that you are making if you were on the other side of the table? If you have any doubt at all, then it is likely that your prospect doesn't or won't believe your presentation either.

The problem is twofold. First, you are the expert on your products and services. You know the value of your product as it relates to your prospect's issues, pains, and goals. (We are assuming that you have done the work to create a value inventory and have correlated value with the C-Suite metrics.) The fact that you are the expert is both a blessing and a curse, because you will not always seem like a credible source when you are demonstrating the value that your products bring to the table. Remember, you are there with the prospect for the opportunity to *sell* your products and services; this in itself diminishes your credibility. To improve your credibility, we suggest that your presentation include current customer success stories or case studies, expert research from outside firms like those mentioned in the previous section (such as Gartner Group, Forrester Research, or Aberdeen), and as much of your prospect's validated data and input as possible.

The second problem is the C-Suite effect itself. Are you qualified to provide information that relates to the financial health of an organization? Your credibility will be challenged at every turn when you begin to discuss topics like earnings; earnings before interest, taxes, depreciation, and amortization (EBITDA); net profit; return on assets (ROA); or return on equity (ROE) with a C-level executive. You must thoroughly understand these concepts and your product's impact on each of the C-Suite metrics. If you are uncomfortable with these topics, go to your company's CFO and ask for a lesson on the impact of your product on C-Suite metrics as they relate to your value inventory matrix. It is not unusual for the CFO of a small company to be involved in the sales process if need be. In larger firms, financial experts and support personnel are generally available to the sales force for support.

Again, the use of outside research when presenting your value is very effective. These firms independently research a variety of subjects. For example, one of our customers, Planview, sells project portfolio management (PPM) systems. These systems help large IT departments to manage their resources better. Forrester Research performed a study discussing the impact of using PPM on large IT departments and the potential benefits these departments will realize. Planview often cites this study during the sales process as a reference to how PPM can have a positive impact on an organization's IT performance.

Of course, most of the research is not free. You will have to pay for the final report. You may also have to pay to use the data in your sales cycle. There is a web site we like a lot, www.Bitpipe.com, where you can research a variety of subjects and receive white papers at no charge. The best part about this web site is that the data are available by industry and/or keywords. You enter the search criteria, and Bitpipe presents you with all of the papers available that match your keywords.

There are several reports available from one or more of these research firms on just about every industry topic, issue, or pain. Another opportunity for research results is doing a survey of your own customers. Here are a few guidelines on surveying your customer base:

- Use your discovery questions as a guide to creating survey questions.

- Identify a sampling of customers who will participate.

- Offer the results to participants for free.

- Set up precise times to discuss the questions, and agree to stick to a time limit.

- Interview your customers, document their answers, and average those answers for final results.

- Publish an internal document that you can share with management, Sales, and Marketing.

KEY POINT

You have at your fingertips a great resource in your own customer base. Companies spend millions of dollars each year sending their sales staffs for training to learn to sell, and yet they rarely spend time or resources on understanding why customers buy and the value that they receive.

Once you have your report published internally, you can then refer to this survey as a research report and share the results with prospects. This concept adds to the credibility of your presentation because you are able to "prove" your value proposition through your own customer base.

Ask yourself these questions to see how credible your presentation is:

- Did we use reliable, high-quality research to validate our findings and recommendations?

- Are the sales tools that we used to collect our prospects' data objective?

- Did we completely document our process and findings when collecting data for a presentation?

We believe it is necessary to answer yes to each of these questions. If you cannot, you are putting the credibility of your sales tools in danger by creating the risk that they will not be accepted as valid by the very prospects you are using them on.

Credibility is one of the most important factors in the presentation process. Remember to keep your opinions to yourself during pain discovery. Present the findings in a way that relies on fact, research, and/or customer surveys. Use phrases like, "Our research with our customer base indicates . . ." or "According to a Gartner Group study last year . . ."

Finally, we are often asked about creating sales tools in-house versus outsourcing the development. If you are diligent in remaining objective during your development process and projecting credibility, you should be able to create tools that your sales force can use with confidence. It is crucial, however, that you be able to explain the process, outlining the extent of the efforts that went into it, in order to drive objectivity and credibility.

ACCURACY

This should go without saying, but the accuracy of your presentation will obviously have a great deal of impact on your credibility. Here is a checklist of items that you must ensure are accurate and take into account when building a credible and objective presentation:

- Math is checked, double-checked, and then checked again.

- Spelling is correct.

- The industry vernacular is used properly.

- Graphs are properly prepared—check for proper spacing of your numbers.

- A glossary is implemented to explain terms.

- Calculations are explained. Whenever possible, show the calculation used or document the calculation nearby.

- The logo is the correct size and colors.

- The font is consistent and easy to read.

- Page breaks line up properly.

- Capitalization, punctuation, and fonts are used properly.

- There is proper data-collection flow—ensure that your presentation flows logically. (Test it out on your CFO before presenting it to a prospect.)

Accuracy involves more than just the spelling and the math. You must consider all the pieces of your presentation. We can't tell you how many presentations we have reviewed that were confusing, ugly, and downright impossible to understand. Stay away from PowerPoint presentations that drone on, ROI tools that are impossible to decipher, and proposals that include a hundred pages of minutiae. Ask yourself, "Could a high school senior understand this?" If the answer is yes, then you are on your way. If not, start over at the beginning of this chapter.

GRAPHICS

It's true that "a picture is worth a thousand words." We strongly suggest that you integrate several charts and graphs throughout your sales tools. Display results along the way. Bar charts, pie charts, and line graphs are all effective tools for a presentation. However, keep your charts simple. Too often we overthink a chart and end up with something that only a Harvard MBA could read and understand. We are fond of using some of the unique charts that Microsoft Excel has to offer. (See Figure 7-2.)

A simple bar chart that is enhanced by using black and white, with backup data shown below the chart, is very effective and dramatic. Another chart we are fond of that offers some interesting graphics that will get a lot of attention is shown in Figure 7-3. This is a 3D chart with a picture in the background. Here we simply used a picture of money as the background to draw attention to the graph.

FIGURE 7-2

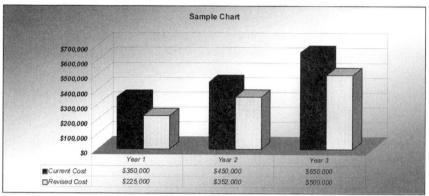

FIGURE 7-3

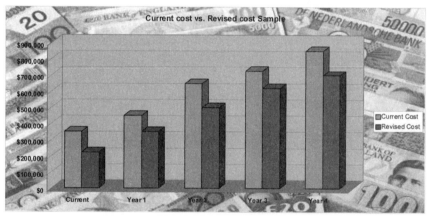

Although this graph is difficult to read, it is effective in making the point that there is a reduction in the cost. Placing a picture in the background of a graph is an effective way to "spice up" the presentation.

Keep in mind that color is an important part of graphic presentations. Use appealing colors that blend well together.

EDUCATIONAL CONTENT

When we ask sales professionals, "What is your job?" we generally get responses such as: "I am supposed to sell our goods and services" or "I am supposed to work my sales plan." These responses are true on the surface, but they don't spell out the entire picture. We feel that the sales process is also supposed to be educational.

Too often, your prospects (and customers, too) don't understand the value that you are trying to deliver to them. They only know their issues and have some idea as to what they want in order to resolve them. This is sometimes overlooked in the sales process. Your literature, seminars, and pain-discovery questions are all directed at educating the prospect as you work through his buying process and your sales cycle. This is vital to the success of the sale. It will help mitigate risk later and also establish expectations for after the sale. Here are the questions you will want to ask yourself when determining if you are educating your prospects effectively:

- Do my pain-discovery questions and the subsequent presentation educate the buyers? Have I clearly defined what it is that the buyers are supposed to have learned from our discussion?

- Does my presentation output inform buyers of what to expect after the sale?

- Do I use marketing information (statistics, research, customer information, social proof, and so on) as an integral part of my presentation?

Be sure you have answered yes to all of these questions. When we interview our customers regarding their presentations, the most common response is something like this: "When we present our findings and demonstrate our value, prospects sometimes just don't seem to get it. We believe our value proposition is simple and easy to understand. It should be clear to prospects how we can provide solutions to their problems."

When you are educating a buyer, you have to lay out your business case in a way that tells the whole story, from pain identification to result measurement. This is a 360-degree approach to resolving a prospect's problem. Too often, presentations are simply about solutions. The problem with this is that prospects forget the issues, pains, and goals that you discussed and agreed upon early in the sales cycle. Now you are weeks, months, or perhaps years into a sale, and your prospects have forgotten, given up on, or changed their pain priority. A better approach is to continually confirm their issues with output from your questionnaire, discuss the impact on their organization, and then present a solution. This way, you are educating buyers along the way and gaining agreement that their issues, pains, and goals still exist, and that resolving them is a priority. This approach will ensure that your presentation is on target and your value message is accepted.

When you create output for your presentation and throughout the sales process, it should maintain all of the attributes that we discussed at the beginning of this chapter, including credibility, objectivity, accuracy, graphics, educational content, and the C-Suite effect. Be sure that you include a synopsis of the information you have collected to date. In addition to the summary, be sure to present and discuss the future cost and value delivered.

The last question we had you ask yourself is focused on proving your value in the presentation. Earlier in the book, we discussed several ways in which you prove that you can deliver value. In your presentation, however, it is crucial that you include social proof, such as reliable expert results from independent firms like Gartner Group or Forrester Research, or your own customer survey results. The problem you face lies in who makes up the audience. Often your presentation is made before executives whom you have not met or had an opportunity to bond with. When you present social proof, it provides a foundation for credibility. Customer quotes, case studies, and referrals are almost always the best social proof you can provide.

We would like to make one last point about educating a prospect. Too often we lose to the status quo because those whom we believe are truly prospects end up not being prospects at all. They are simply fishing for information. During the discovery phase of your sales process, you need to determine who is real and who is not. Be sure to include questions that will reveal a prospect's true intent.

BOTH VALUE AND COSTS PRESENTED

Sales professionals can get caught up in the value side of the presentation and forget that there is a cost side, too. When presenting value, you must provide your prospect with both sides of the equation. If you are using value estimation tools like ROI, then as part of the process, you will already be estimating the costs as they relate to the value returned. If not, however, you will need to identify and capture the investment required as part of your presentation.

One of the most commonly overlooked issues is that cost does not stop with the initial investment. No matter what the product, there are ongoing costs associated with the ongoing benefits. If you do not show the ongoing costs completely and accurately over a period of time, you lose the credibility attached to the overall benefit. We suggest that you look at the costs and benefits over at least the next three years. Remember, the only way to understand your prospects' threshold for pain (the point at which they make a decision based on pain outweighing benefit) is to help them capture and calculate the future cost and expected value over a three- to seven-year period.

Once you are able to identify, confirm, and present both the pain and the value delivered, your next discussion should be about identifying the current C-Suite metrics. In other words, capture the data that identify your prospect's current net profit margin, earnings, payroll as a percentage of sales, and so on. Once you have your baseline defined, use the estimated value that your prospect provided to calculate the impact on the C-Suite metrics.

The presentation of this information must be both textual and graphical. Graphics enable your prospect to glance at a document or slide and provide an immediate reaction to the impact. She is likely to want to drill down deeper into how you came to these conclusions. Figure 7-4 provides an example of how to display a C-Suite impact.

FIGURE 7-4

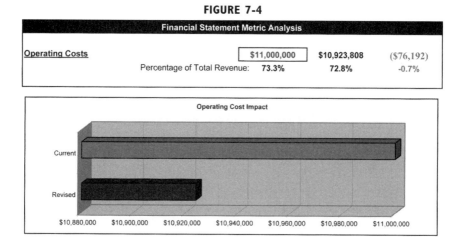

Figure 7-4 displays the impact on operating costs. The prospect's current operating costs are $11 million, or 73.3 percent of total revenue. The revised operating costs are a 0.7 percent reduction, as displayed under the "change" heading in the right-hand column. It may not seem like much of an impact; however, the difference is $76,192. Since you display the impact both textually and graphically, your prospect is able to quickly see the impact (graphically) and read the detail (textually) above it.

There are many ways to display your value; here are some examples of ways in which we have presented our findings.

Figure 7-5 is an example of a graph that includes year-over-year cost, return, net return, and a cumulative return. In addition, we added a line chart to display the cumulative cost versus the cumulative return. As you can see from the chart, the break-even point is around Year 2.

Figure 7-6 includes a year-over-year analysis. We looked at the current year cost and estimated the value that we could deliver by category of value. It's important to show each year because this makes the point that if

FIGURE 7-5

	Year 1	Year 2	Year 3	Summary Total
Investment:	$1,113,000	$306,500	$181,500	$1,601,000
Return:	$598,764	$2,782,205	$6,414,292	$9,795,261
Net Return:	($514,236)	$2,475,705	$6,232,792	
Cumulative Return:	($514,236)	$1,961,469	$8,194,261	$8,194,261

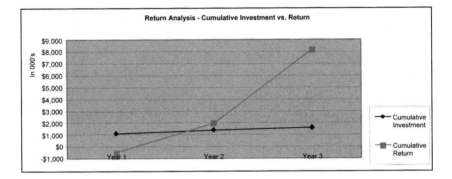

the prospect does nothing (maintains the status quo), there is an ongoing, or rising, cost. As you can see, for each year of maintaining the status quo, the cost increases. In the charts that accompany this display, we include a category chart based on totals that show current value versus revised value delivered over a three-year period. The line chart to the right of the text displays how costs continue to rise. Take note of how the lines begin to separate at the three-year mark. This is typical because once you implement cost-saving measures, the ripple effect will eventually increase the value delivered beyond your initial estimates.

Here are some questions to ask yourself as they relate to the value versus costs equation displayed in your presentation:

- Do we capture the initial and ongoing costs associated with the purchase of our products and/or services?

- Do we effectively show the value delivered, taking into account the initial cost, ongoing cost, and overall benefit delivered?

- Are we able to relate our value to the C-Suite metrics?

FIGURE 7-6

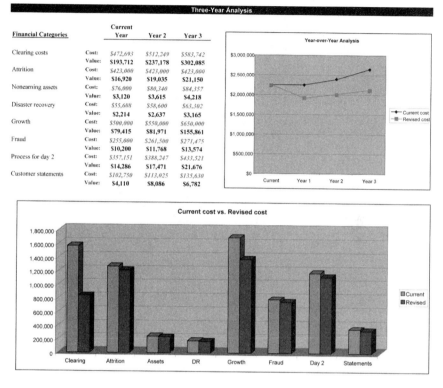

CREATIVE OUTPUT

The success or failure of your presentation boils down to the things we have discussed thus far. Credibility and objectivity are, of course, of primary concern; however, your ability to present the results in a way that helps your prospect believe in them and clearly understand the potential value that you can deliver is equally important. A giant step in accomplishing this is to create an output document that:

- Summarizes the prospect's answers to your questions
- Graphically displays the results
- Includes "industry acceptable" metrics
- Includes the C-Suite effect based on value delivered

- Helps your prospect understand that there is a cost to the status quo

- Is visually appealing and easy to understand (not intimidating)

- Is accurate (math, spelling, vernacular, and so on)

- Includes the initial cost and the ongoing cost of the status quo

- Provides a summary of investment and return

Equally important to the output document is how you present it. We strongly suggest that you connect your output document to a slide presentation explaining the various sections in detail. By using a slide presentation in the proposal stage of the sales process, you are creating an event. This event takes on purpose and positions you better than most competitors. Even if you use one of the online presentation companies like GoToMeeting, WebEx, or Adobe Connect, your presentation of your proposal and value estimation drives you closer to adding this prospect to your customer list.

Keep your slide show simple and to the point. The biggest mistake we see is including too much information on each PowerPoint slide. Once again, graphics are a nice addition, but don't overuse them. It gets to be distracting and annoying if you keep leaving the interpretation up to the prospect by presenting a graphic without an explanation. It is equally distracting to have to verbally explain a complicated graphic to the prospect.

C-SUITE EFFECT

Presenting the C-Suite effect can sometimes be a daunting task. The biggest issue you are likely to face is collecting the baseline information. Keep in mind that if your prospect is a publicly held firm, the data are readily available in public records through financial reports and the prospect's web site.

If your prospect is not a publicly held company, you will be forced to ask, estimate, or use comparisons from existing customers. Once you have committed to using the C-Suite metrics in your sales process, the presentation of the information collected is vital to your success.

Throughout this chapter, we have provided examples of C-Suite presentation material. The bottom line is this: You must display the prospect's current situation and your impact as it relates to each of the metrics. Use your CFO to help you with this process if you are unable to understand the complete impact of your product or service. Here are some additional examples of presenting the C-Suite effect.

Figure 7-7 displays an array of C-Suite metrics in the form of bar or cone graphs. The textual details are displayed above or below the graph for reference.

FIGURE 7-7

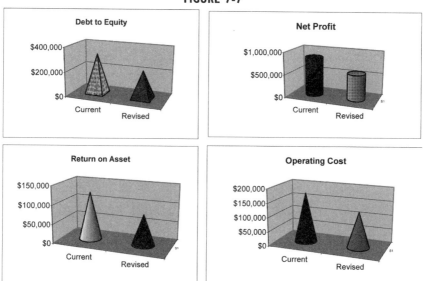

Figure 7-7 provides a textual and graphical view of the metrics. We developed only one graph to display the net change in the metrics. This graph is a nice way to get a quick view of the impact that you will have on the C-Suite metrics. Notice that in Figure 7-8 we have included "planned" expenditures in the operating cost metric, too.

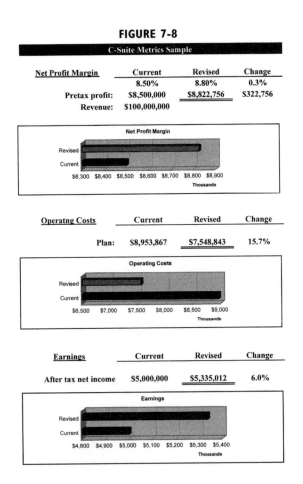

FIGURE 7-8

Another way to display these metrics is in one chart showing only the net changes (see Figure 7-9). We should caution you on creating only summary charts; you may be challenged on the details that led to the changes in the C-Suite metrics.

FIGURE 7-9

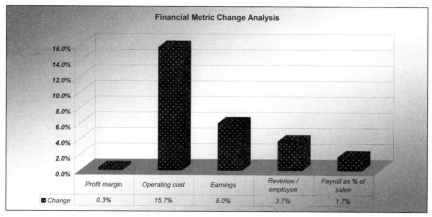

SUMMARY

Over the years, we have learned one thing for sure about presentations: A bad one is likely to cost you the sale. We covered many topics in this chapter to help you with your presentation of the material, including:

- Create a solid foundation based on credibility and objectivity.

- Include social proof in your discussion.

- "Ask!" don't "Tell!"

- Always confirm that your prospect understands and agrees with your assumptions, findings, and statements.

- Be accurate (need we say more?).

The presentation of the data you have gathered is a key component to winning more opportunities. Remember, when you are building your presentation, a picture truly is worth a thousand words. In earlier chapters, we discussed the need to identify pain, capture current and ongoing costs, and estimate value. Each of these steps must be represented in your presentation. In other words, the whole process must be presented and discussed. In addition, the final presentation of the C-Suite metrics and how your products or services affect their movement must be delivered with confidence, credibility, and objectivity.

Besides the need for credibility and objectivity, you must include accurate data that have been checked, double-checked, and triple-checked. If there is a mistake, the entire document is going to be discredited and probably thrown out.

We discussed the need for educational content. Your discovery process will be the litmus test on whether a prospect is real or not. Sometimes prospects are just fishing for information and looking for you to give away some free consulting and education. However, once you have qualified your prospect, your presentation must include material and information that will educate the buyer on your proposed solution. Prospects must feel comfortable that you fully understand their problems and have a solution that will either reduce their costs or increase their revenues.

In the next chapter, we walk you through building your final document: the business case. We turn our focus once again to the C-Suite metrics. If you are unclear as to what the metrics we have defined are or the calculations for each metric, we suggest that you return to earlier chapters and review the metrics and their definitions.

BUILDING YOUR
BUSINESS CASE

We have spent the first seven chapters of this book getting to this point. Building your business case is a key success factor in selling complex goods and services. It must encompass all of your work with your prospect and provide a compelling story that says, "Buy from me, and buy from me now!" A business case is the document that you will ultimately use to present your solution. It should include all of your research, findings from discovery, expectations, and recommendations.

A high-quality business case will consist of many sections that display information that you have collected, calculated, forecasted, and projected. In this chapter, we will cover eight sections that we believe to be the most important. This is not to say that these eight sections are all that should be included. Feel free to add specific product or company information that you feel will enhance your business case document. We are trying to provide a baseline that you can use to establish a high-quality business case model. In Chapter 6 ("Creating a Financial Dashboard"), we had you establish the groundwork for building your business case. Much of the data collected in earlier exercises is used in the business case document.

To be successful selling in the business-to-business (B2B) world using value, you must present a credible and compelling business case analysis model. This analysis must include at the very least the following sections:

- Business case summary results
- C-Suite effect
- Expected value delivered each year (impact)
- Current cost and extrapolated cost over a three- to seven-year period
- Estimated return on investment (ROI), net present value (NPV), internal rate of return (IRR), and payback period (including start-up time)
- Cost of decision delay and cost of no decision
- Cash flow analysis and impact
- Comparison of financial metrics to industry norms
- Investment breakdown

Each of these sections will drive a different discussion with C-level executives. A thorough understanding of each section is necessary to present a high-quality business case model. In this chapter, we define each section, explain its importance, and provide some examples that you can use to build your business case model.

(*Note:* When you submit a document that gives this much information, it is to your advantage to be able to walk the prospect through your findings. Unfortunately, this is not always possible, so the document must provide as complete a picture of your business case as possible. Think of it as a stand-in for you, if necessary, presenting all of your research, findings from discovery, expectations, recommendations, and, finally, your solution, in a clear, concise format.)

BUSINESS CASE SUMMARY RESULTS

If you have followed the instructions from the beginning of Chapter 1, you know that there is a lot of work involved in collecting the information needed to present a high-quality business case. You have researched your prospects; identified their issues, pains, and goals; helped them with their threshold-for-pain decision; and discussed the C-Suite impact of your solution. However, the information you have so painstakingly collected doesn't exactly tell the whole story on its own. You must pull all the data together in one location and analyze them, taking each of the pieces into account. If you don't do this, it would be like writing a book and leaving out some of the chapters. The business case is used to pull all the pieces together and provide you with an opportunity to present the whole picture to the prospect from beginning to end in one document.

Often your business case will be seen by people you may never have met before. When it comes time to present your findings to these people, the material that you have collected may be incomplete. The first few pages of the business case document should be a summary of everything that you have accomplished *to this point* in the sale. It must include your process, findings, results, and recommendations. The format is up to you. However, we have some thoughts and ideas to share with you.

Many of our customers used to simply print a copy of the financial dashboard and give it to their customers. We don't do this because the financial dashboard is not designed to explain the process and all of the recommendations you are making to the prospect. The financial dashboard and the business case should be used and presented at different points in the sales process. Think of it this way: When you first meet your prospect, do you provide him with a proposal? Of course not! A proposal has a place in the process; if it is provided too soon, you will lose some of your ability to sell.

Finally, your business case is a story with a beginning, a middle, and an end. The story begins by uncovering and exposing your prospect's issues, pains, and goals. The middle part, or the meat of the story, is a journey into the cost of maintaining the status quo and the prospect's threshold for pain. The conclusion of your story begins with the financial dashboard and C-Suite impact, and ends with the business case and demonstration of your value.

The summary page of your business case should include the following:

- Introduction
    - Details on your process for collecting the data
    - Assumptions made (if any)
    - Summary results
    - Goals going forward
    - Sections that follow
    - Number of years the business case covers
    - Overview sections for
        - C-Suite effect
        - Investment
        - Issues defined
            - Current cost
            - Estimated value
        - Cash flow
        - Cost of status quo and no decision
        - Multiyear impact and analysis

We suggest that you begin with a couple of paragraphs that explain the business case model and what your expectation is for delivery. (See Figure 8-1.) On the introduction page, we have included four sections: process, results, goals, and a preview of what is included in the rest of the document. In this case, we didn't make any assumptions during data collection, so we excluded that section. Remember that this is only an example of a summary page. You may want to add additional information for discussion.

FIGURE 8-1

Business Case Analysis - Introduction

Prepared For: ABC Enterprises   March 30, 2010

The following business case analysis is prepared by us to incorporate research conducted based on defined issues, pains, and goals. We surveyed your organization to determine primary (pain) issues. We next captured and calculated your current cost of status quo and extrapolated that cost over a three year period based on your estimated future growth. Once we demonstrated the value proposition, together we determined the estimated value that our products and services could provide your organization. The estimates for value and growth were discussed and agreed upon during the proof of concept phase of the process.

Process

Please review each section of the business case to determine the overall effect on your organization and in terms of the following: (1) Current cost of the status quo; (2) extrapolated cost over the three year period; (3) cost of implementing a new solution, and (4) estimated value delivered over the three year analysis period. There are several sections to this document you may want to explore during your review, beginning with the C-Suite effect. This section helps you determine our impact on your financial metrics like profit, earnings, and operating costs. Next we provide a three year analysis of cost and estimated value, followed by details for impact on revenue increases and cost reduction. In addition we break out your investment and cash flow over a three year period for you to determine where the costs are being allocated.

Results

Our process determined that there are issues in the following area:

- Excessive discounting
- Customer attrition
- Ever increasing new hire costs

We have determined with the help of your team that we are able to improve your revenue results by as much as 5% due to a major reduction in discounting and attrition. In addition your new hire cost and training are affected by our follow up programs that will continually engage your team in online training.

Goals

Part of the ROI Selling process is to establish two sets of goals. One, for the next twelve months and one for the next three years. We have established increases in revenue by up to 8% due to the reduction in discounting and attrition and operating cost reduction by invoking better hiring practices. In the first year strides are expected to be made in all three areas to amount to a minimum increase in revenue of one million dollars. In addition we expect to cut our hiring costs by up to 9% annually. This 9% will increase to 25% over the next three years.

Section that follow

- Project overview and summary   - Issues, pains and goals

- C-Suite impact   - Multiple year analysis

- Investment guidelines   - Status quo summary

- Cash flow analysis   - Recommendations

Project Financial Summary

Following the introduction, we suggest that you include the project overview and summary page. This page will display much of the data that you have collected during the discovery phase of the sales process, but only in a summary format. It will also include all of your financial dashboard inputs, such as investment information, decision delay, C-Suite metrics, and current status. Figure 8-2 is an example of a summary page that we designed for one of our customers. (*Note:* We removed their logos for privacy.) You should include your logo on each page of the business case document. Notice that we have included sections on the first-year investment and return; project investment and return; cash flow summary; C-Suite summary, current and revised; and status quo summary.

FIGURE 8-2

ABC Enterprises   January 2, 2009

This dashboard is used to consolidate data and provide the baseline information needed to create a compelling business case. The analysis below consists of financial summary information, investment information, and status quo costs. As with any dashboard, we require input and provide informative output that you can use to assess your current situation and estimate the value we are capable of delivering.

First-Year Financial Summary (Risk Adjusted)	
First-Year Investment:	$900,000
First-Year Impact:	($643,000)

First-Year Category Summary (Risk Adjusted)	
Impact from Cost Reductions:	$225,000
Impact from Revenue Increases:	$82,700
External Savings Estimated:	$57,300

Project Financial Summary (Risk Adjusted)	
Total Investment:	$1,638,000
Total Impact: (Risk Adjusted)	$2,594,000
Return on Investment:	158%
Payback Period: (Months)	22.7
Net Present Value:	$737,620
Internal Rate of Return:	48%

Cash Flow Summary	
Number of years included:	3 years
Investment:	$1,638,000
Return: (Risk Adjusted)	$2,594,000
Cumulative Return:	$956,000

C-Suite Summary		
C-Suite Category	Current	Revised
Net Profit Margin:	$2,400,000	$2,582,439
Operating Costs:	$11,000,000	$10,858,704
Sales / Employee:	$3,000,000	$3,228,049
Payroll as Percentage of Sales:	25.0%	22.9%
Earnings:	$2,400,000	$2,407,119

Investment Summary	
Hardware	$500,000
Software	$460,000
Consulting	$100,000
Maintenance	$200,000
Internal costs	$225,000
Upgrades	$90,000
Materials	$45,000
Miscellaneous	$3,000
Other	$15,000

Status Quo Summary	
Three-year cost of status quo:	$6,750,000
Daily cost of status quo:	$8,654
Revised daily cost of status quo:	$4,308
Decision delay cost:	$134,769

Each section of the business case is represented on this summary page. Following the summary, it is suggested that you include a detailed analysis of each section to review with your customer. Following are examples of details that we have included in this business case model.

First-Year Financial Analysis

The first-year financial summary is a breakdown of each of the primary discovery areas, displayed to include the current cost, revised cost, and estimated value delivered or your prospect's goal for the project. We recommend that you also include a short paragraph explaining your value and what your prospect should expect once you have implemented your solution. This is important because it enables you to manage your prospect's expectations and continue to stay on the same page. Each section is represented by a financial category. For example, in Figure 8-3, we display the details for cost reductions. You will want to include similar details for revenue increases and cost avoidances. Remember, each section must tell a story. We include a graphic like a bar chart to help enhance the story and make it easier to understand.

C-SUITE EFFECT

The foundation or highlight of your business case model is the C-Suite effect. The C-Suite effect is a key component because your prospect will have the ability to monitor your impact on a regular basis. ROI is typically measured (or not) long after the project has been paid for, implemented, and deployed. You now have the opportunity to work with your prospect to define the expected results and work within the organization to track and monitor your successes.

Return to your value inventory and confirm that you have correlated the value with the key metrics that we discussed in Chapter 1. This exercise should be done with a qualified financial expert, such as your company's CFO. Once you have successfully assigned each value you deliver to an impact on one or more financial levers, you are ready to sell to the C-Suite. Your presentation of the information is the key to a successful sale. In Chapter 7, we displayed several screen prints for a presentation. The following is a detailed explanation of the C-Suite metrics used by one of our customers. We begin with a sample presentation (Figure 8-4) of the C-Suite effect.

FIGURE 8-3

Business Case Analysis - First Year Analysis			

Cost Reductions	Current Cost	Revised Cost	Value Delivered
Annual FTE cost reduction from reducing number of days less productive new hires remain on staff:	$173,077	$69,231	$103,846

Research indicates that 82% of newly hired sales professionals are a mistake. A mistake is defined as: (a) The individual leaves the organization within two years because of his or her own lack of satisfaction, (b) you terminate him or her due to your lack of satisfaction with his or her performance, and (c) the worst scenario, the sales professional is still there, but you wish he or she wasn't. We provide a methodology that includes an assessment that ensures that your hires are high quality, productive, and continually produce year after year.

	Current Cost	Revised Cost	Value Delivered
Annual startup and recruiting cost reduction:	$53,500	$16,050	$37,450

By implementing better hiring practices you are able to reduce the amount of time, effort, and money spent on recruiting additional personnel. Once we reduce your turnover, retain your team longer, and improve their performance you are able to see the results in less recruiting costs, reduced training expenses, and increases in revenue each year.

	Current Cost	Revised Cost	Value Delivered
Cost reduction from reducing number of days to close a sale:	$6,300,000	$5,372,237	$927,763

A common concern of many executives is that as their sales volume increases, their margins will decrease. Our trained sales professionals not only sell more, but they also get higher margins. While we certainly focus on increasing sales volume, we never forget about that other critical element--maintaining or increasing margins--that has a multiplying effect on the bottom-line results.

Summary Total of Value Delivered:	$6,526,577	$5,457,518	$1,069,059

In Figure 8-4, net profit margin is a metric that is affected by increases in revenue and reductions in most costs. The calculation for net profit margin is net pretax profit divided by revenue. That being said, any effect that you have on revenue will affect net profit margin. For example, if your prospect's current net profit margin is 8.3 percent and its revenues are $100 million, then its pretax profit is $8,300,000. If you can increase revenue by 3 percent, from $100 million to $103 million, then the result will be $249,000 in additional net profit.

FIGURE 8-4

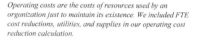

Business Case Analysis - Financial Metrics (First year only)

Net profit impact was affected by multiple line items in the financial model, including all revenue increases and cost reductions described in detail in this business case.

Operating costs are the costs of resources used by an organization just to maintain its existence. We included FTE cost reductions, utilities, and supplies in our operating cost reduction calculation.

Net profit

Current net profit	8.0%	$2,400,000
Revised profit margin	8.3%	$2,496,914

Operating costs

Current operating cost	$11,000,000	36.7%
Revised operating cost	$9,930,941	33.1%

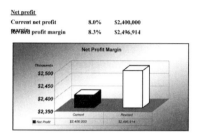

Sales per employee is an indicator of where you can do more with less personnel costs. We provide this ratio to help with understanding financial health and productivity.

Controlling payroll is a critical success factor for most companies. This metric will help us gauge company growth by tracking the relationship between payroll and revenue.

Sales per employee

Current sales / employee	$300,000
Revised sales / employee	$321,000

Payroll as percentage of sales

Current payroll	$7,500,000	25.0%
Revised payroll	$7,396,154	22.9%

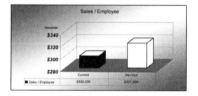

The point of this exercise is simple. By adding $3.0 million in revenue, the impact is a 3 percent increase in net profit. You now have more of a story to tell than just "increase in revenue" or ROI.

EXPECTED VALUE DELIVERED EACH YEAR (IMPACT)

Most prospects expect a proposal that outlines their cost to purchase over a period of years. This is used primarily for planning cash flow. Your business case should include the expected impact that your products or services will have over the same period of time. Figure 8-5 provides a breakdown of the extrapolated costs and impacts that you created earlier in the process. The display is used to prompt a discussion of the threshold for pain. We include graphics and call-outs to help with the interpretation of the data. For example, on the first graph, we added a call-out to draw the customer's attention to the fact that, as the project continues, the goal line is separating from the status quo line. Thus, costs will continue to be reduced at a more rapid rate than the rising status quo line.

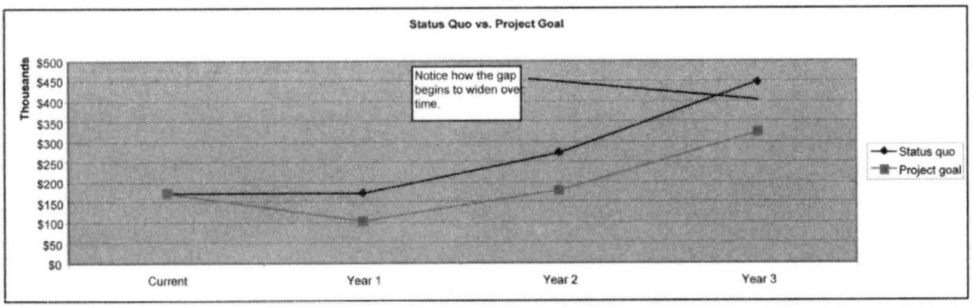

FIGURE 8-5

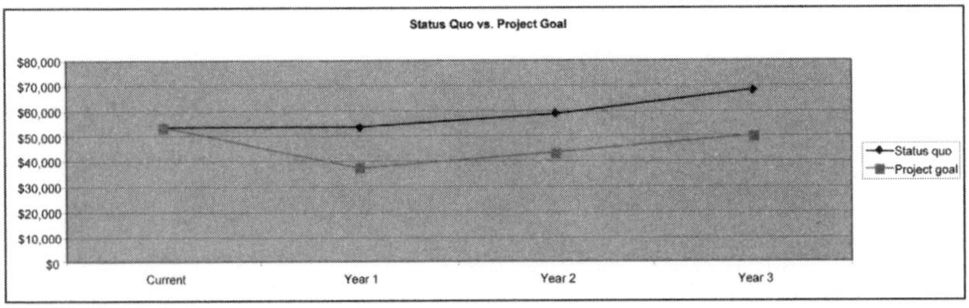

CURRENT COST AND EXTRAPOLATED COST
OVER A THREE- TO SEVEN-YEAR PERIOD

In Figure 8-5, you will notice that each chart is showing the current year cost, Year 2 cost, and Year 3 cost. These graphs incorporate the concept of "status quo is not free." In other words, if the prospect decides to do nothing about the pains defined, here is a chart showing what the cost/pain will do over time. This chart can be extrapolated out as many years as you feel are necessary. We typically use a three-year period for software; however, many sales organizations project cost and value out seven years.

ESTIMATED ROI, NPV, IRR, AND PAYBACK PERIOD

Financial metrics are "expected" to be provided in every business case document. The challenge you will face is making sure that they are credible. The math is very simple and straightforward. For example, ROI is total impact divided by total investment. As stated earlier, the problem with ROI is: How believable is it? We feel that ROI needs to be displayed, but you should be aware that it is likely to be ignored as a metric of value.

Net present value (NPV) is defined as the difference between the present value of the cash inflows and the present value of the cash outflows. NPV is used in capital budgeting to analyze the profitability of an investment. More simply, it compares the value of a dollar today to the value of that same dollar in the future, taking into account inflation and returns. If the NPV is positive, your solution should be accepted; if it is negative, however, the investment is likely to be rejected for causing negative cash flows.

NPV is expected to be included in most business case models. However, the actual calculation will probably be done by the CFO of the buying organization because value estimates coming from a vendor may not be considered trustworthy in the minds of the C-Suite executives.

Internal rate of return measures and compares the profitability of an investment. Sometimes IRR is referred to as the discounted cash flow rate, or simply the rate of return. When used in your business case, the IRR is an indicator of the efficiency, quality, or yield of an investment. This is in contrast to NPV, which is an indicator of the value of an investment.

If the IRR is greater than the established acceptable rate of return, then it is considered acceptable. (Usually the acceptable rate of return is the cost to acquire.) It is not unusual for a prospect to look at multiple investments with different costs side by side, based on the IRR, when making some buying decisions. IRR is typically included in a business case model. Again, the final calculation will probably be performed by the CFO of the buying company, but your calculations will be viewed as a guideline based on the information you had available at the time you developed the business case model.

Payback period refers to the period of time required for the return on an investment to "repay" the total original investment. For example, an investment of $100 that returns $20 per year would have a five-year payback period. The goal is to have a short payback period. We usually extend the payback period in our models by the number of months needed for start-up. In other words, don't start figuring the payback until your solution will be fully operational and the prospect will start reaping the benefit of the investment. Be careful when including payback period in your business case, because if the returns are not accurate, the result of the calculation is going to be wrong.

We display these calculations only on the summary page. There is not really any need to create detail pages for ROI, NPV, IRR, and payback period.

COST OF DECISION DELAY AND COST OF NO DECISION

Remember this statement: The status quo is not free! If you are able to articulate this concept, buying decisions will be forthcoming. This very simple calculation is used to help your prospect understand that there is a cost to sitting on the sidelines.

We must again begin with your pain-discovery questions. You must identify pain, capture and calculate the current and ongoing cost of the status quo, and estimate your value over a three- to seven-year period. Figure 8-6 shows the way we like to display it.

FIGURE 8-6

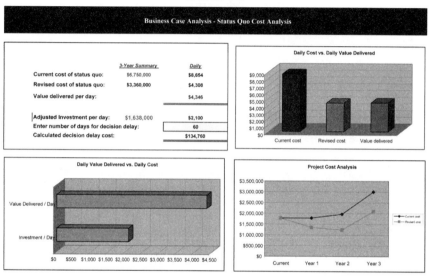

In the first column, we display all of the costs we captured during the discovery phase of the sales process. We next divide the $6,750,000 by three years and then by the number of working days in a year (260). This results in a current daily cost of $8,654. Below the current cost figure, we capture all of the estimated values or goals we defined that were related to cost reductions and display them below the $6,750,000. Next, we divide the $3,360,000 by three years and 260 days. That gives us a revised cost of status quo of $4,308. Subtracting $4,308 from $8,654 results in a figure of $4,346, the value delivered per day.

Value, of course, is not free. You must now add in the cost to acquire the value, or the investment, that you are asking your prospect to make. The math is exactly the same. Add up the cost over the same period of time ($1,638,000) and divide by the number of years (three) and then by the number of working days per year (260). This calculation will give you the daily cost of the investment: $2,100.

When you subtract the investment per day ($2,100) from the expected value delivered per day ($4,346), you will get the true cost of the status quo. Think of this exercise as having three components:

1. Cost of doing nothing (the status quo)

2. Value delivered (your value)

3. Cost to receive the value (investment)

In this example, you will notice that we have prospects enter the number of days they expect to take to make a buying decision or purchase (in this case, 60). We then multiply the daily cost of the status quo ($4,346 − $2,100 = $2,246) times the days of decision delay (60) and determine a cost of decision delay. In this example, the 60-day delay is costing more than $134,000. In the business case document, we build graphics around these metrics.

When you develop your business case, be sure to include several graphics for comparisons. We have included three charts that you may want to consider:

1. Daily cost versus daily value delivered. This chart has three parts—the current daily cost, the revised daily cost, and a line displaying the value delivered per day.

2. In the second chart, we show the investment made per day versus the value delivered per day.

3. Finally, we have included a graphic that provides a three-year look at cost versus value delivered.

KEY POINT

The most important thing to remember when developing this section is to be sure that you include only cost line items in the value delivered calculations. Even though revenue lines add value, this section is built around only cost reductions. The reason for this is that with revenue lines, there is no current cost to compare to the value delivered (cost reduction).

If you were successful in identifying pain, capturing and calculating cost, and estimating value during the pain-discovery phase, then these calculations will be very simple. The graphic display gives you an opportunity to discuss the impact that your products or services will have on the investment and what the consequences will be if the prospect does not make the investment. Keep in mind the importance of using your prospect's data in doing your calculations.

CASH FLOW ANALYSIS AND IMPACT

The impact that you will have on the prospect's cash flow can be determined by three common components:

1. Year-over-year investment

2. Year-over-year expected return

3. Cumulative return

We feel that by charting the baseline information and cumulative calculations, you will be able to discuss with your prospects the impact that the investment and return will have each year. If you created your sales tools using a spreadsheet program, be sure to make this section interactive. You will want to be able to enter investment information or value-delivered data and discuss the impact with your prospect. (See Figure 8-7.)

Figure 8-7 shows a three-year cash flow analysis for one of our clients. Note that the first year has a negative return or result. The break-even point is shown at just after Year 2. When discussing this information with your prospect, you should understand how your impact can be accelerated, altered, or increased.

In the second graph, we display the impact goal line on top, followed by the expected cumulative return. When the two lines meet, the goal is achieved. In this example, that will probably occur after Year 3.

FIGURE 8-7

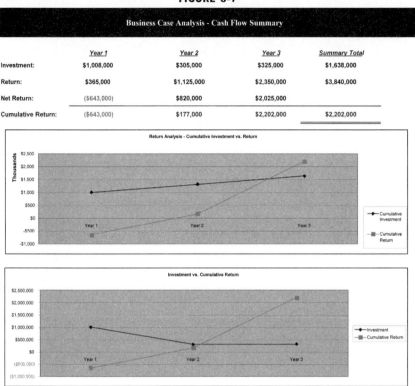

In Chapter 5, we introduced you to a new web site on financial metrics norms by industry from *Inc.* magazine that will provide you with comparison information on the C-Suite metrics. We believe that there is a place in your business case for this information. When you include standards to compare the status quo with, you are providing a service to your prospect. (See Figure 8-8.)

COMPARISON OF FINANCIAL METRICS TO INDUSTRY NORMS

FIGURE 8-8

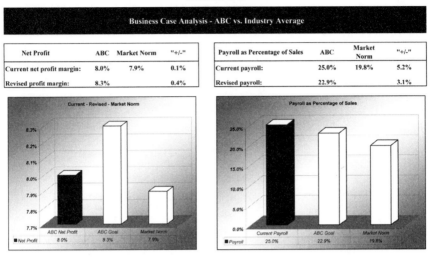

Business Case Analysis - ABC vs. Industry Average

Net Profit	ABC	Market Norm	"+/-"
Current net profit margin:	8.0%	7.9%	0.1%
Revised profit margin:	8.3%		0.4%

Payroll as Percentage of Sales	ABC	Market Norm	"+/-"
Current payroll:	25.0%	19.8%	5.2%
Revised payroll:	22.9%		3.1%

* Industry norms are provided by Sageworks and *Inc.* magazine by industry

INVESTMENT BREAKDOWN

Many companies choose not to break down the investment. Therefore, if you use lump-sum prices or don't use any cost breakdowns, you should skip this section and move on to the summary. The only significant change between the business case and the financial dashboard is the graphic that breaks down the costs in a pie chart. (See Figure 8-9.)

SUMMARY

Your business case could be the most important tool you will use in your sales process. If you fail to collect the data required to complete a high-quality business case, however, the document itself is useless. On the other hand, if you do collect the necessary data and present the information to your prospect, your odds of winning the sale increase significantly.

FIGURE 8-9

Business Case Analysis - Investment Overview

Investment Category	Deposit	Year 1	Year 2	Year 3	Summary Totals
Hardware	$125,000	$125,000	$125,000	$125,000	$500,000
Software	$175,000	$175,000	$50,000	$60,000	$460,000
Consulting		$100,000			$100,000
Maintenance	$50,000	$50,000	$50,000	$50,000	$200,000
Internal costs		$65,000	$75,000	$85,000	$225,000
Upgrades	$90,000				$90,000
Materials	$45,000				$45,000
Miscellaneous		$3,000			$3,000
Other	$5,000		$5,000	$5,000	$15,000
Summary Totals	$490,000	$518,000	$305,000	$325,000	$1,638,000

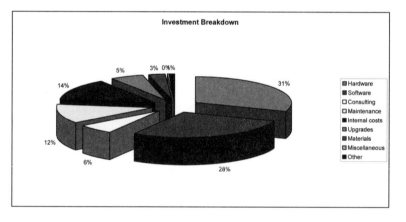

Building your business case means developing a tool that you can use to sell at all levels within an organization. At a minimum, your business case must include the following:

- Summary section—for casual readers to find what they are looking for quickly and easily.

- C-Suite effect—for financial decision makers to weigh the cost against their financial metrics and determine the viability of purchasing from you.

- Expected value delivered each year—for the businesspeople to plan their future hiring, purchasing, and marketing.

- Current cost and extrapolated cost over at least three years—for executives to make informed buying decisions based on cost and value expected over an extended period of time.

- Estimated ROI, NPV, IRR, and payback period—for the CEO, CFO, and COO to compare this investment to other options that are on the table.

- Cost of decision delay and cost of no decision—for all management to realize that the status quo is not free and that decision delay has a cost to it.

- Cash flow analysis—C-level finance people are looking at this on a daily basis. Your output will help them determine the impact on their cash flow over an extended period of time.

- Comparison of financial metrics to industry norms—this is used by executives to determine two things: First, how do we compare to the market? Second, where are our competitors in relation to us on these metrics?

- Investment breakdown—used for cash flow planning by the CFO and the vice president of finance, in addition to the CEO.

The use of a spreadsheet program will make your business case easier to put together and give you the tools to build something more elaborate. There are numerous books on creating graphs and charts in spreadsheet programs. One of my favorites is *Excel Dashboards and Reports* by Michael Alexander (Wiley, 2010). I believe that when you provide discovery results in multiple formats, your prospect will be able to consume the information more easily. Some people like numbers, some like pictures, and others have to hear and see material to absorb it. Be sure to use a variety of charts with color and proper labeling.

WHAT THEY DON'T TEACH YOU IN SALES TRAINING

I wanted to provide you with some real-life insights into how the ideas outlined and discussed in this book can affect your process, your methodology, and your sales success. So I contacted some of my friends, colleagues, and customers and asked them, "What is it that you were not taught in sales training?" Once I received their answers, I applied the concepts and principles from *The Key to the C-Suite* to their comments.

Following are responses from some of the best sales trainers, teachers, authors, and thinkers I have ever met. Some of these responses are short and some are long, but they are all helpful in understanding what's going on in the real world of sales. And they reinforce the concepts discussed in this book.

SALES PROFESSIONALS . . . DO WE REALLY NEED THEM?

Harvey Shovers, President of MSI Data

> *"My comments depend on the industry and the complexity of the sale,*
> *but too often, sales professionals get in the way of a sale. They want to*
> *prove their value and often slow the deal down. A good pre-sales person*
> *is worth five sales professionals. Times have changed; everything is*
> *specialized now. For example, prospecting is done by outside firms or*
> *internal call groups. Proposals are automated or done by a special*
> *department. Pre-sales engineers do all of the demonstrations and gain*
> *the trust of the prospect. Management is needed to close the deal.*
> *Unless you have someone very special (and there are very few of those),*
> *what is the value of the salesperson?"*

Harvey's view may be a bit harsh—but often true—when it comes to
the need for sales professionals, but it doesn't have to apply to you. You can
separate yourself from the pack by following the ideas in this book, and if
you do, your value as a sales professional will be unquestioned.

Chapter 1 teaches you a language that will become very useful when
you are talking to C-Suite executives. The financial metrics that we define
there and later associate with your value (Chapter 2) will provide you with
insight that the "average" sales professional will never have. Later, when we
discuss financial reports (Chapter 4) and research options (Chapter 4),
you will be getting an education that will make you unique in your
approach and your abilities.

I was talking recently to a customer at Hewlett-Packard (HP). He told
me that he had just returned from special training on reading annual
reports and understanding HP's value and how it affects a company's overall IT budget, which in turn affects its financials and ultimately its annual
report and shareholder value.

When you use the tools we discuss throughout the book, you will
quickly know whether a prospect is truly a prospect. The discovery
required in Chapter 3 forces a prospect to think hard about her business.

It is sort of a built-in qualifying questionnaire. You will gain the ability to discuss your product's financial impact on your prospect's business, interact with key C-level personnel, and collect the necessary data to create a compelling business case. In addition, with all of this knowledge in hand during the presentation, you will be able to focus your team on what is important to the prospect.

GET BUY-IN FROM ALL THE KEY PLAYERS— NOT JUST THE EXECUTIVES

David Hunkele, vice president of sales, S1 Corporation

> *"Armed with only the goal of getting to C-level executives, I learned the hard way that no one likes having a new product jammed down their throat. Most people want to participate in the selection process. Getting the key individuals at all levels to buy in early accelerates the sales process. It is true that executives make the strategic decisions, but key players within the company determine the success or failure of those purchases."*

Developing high-quality discovery questions (Chapters 2 and 3) will ensure that you are working with key personnel throughout your prospect's organization. Remember, it is rare that one individual will have all of the answers to your initial discovery questions. Your questions will not only help you collect the data you need to make recommendations and create a business case (Chapters 7 and 8), but also help you engage with other key players who are involved in strategic buying decisions.

Remember to create output reports (Chapter 7) that you can forward to each contact every time you collect additional discovery information after the initial pain-discovery process takes place. This follow-up and interaction will pay off tenfold when you have your opportunity to meet with C-level executives. Each interaction you have with your prospect's personnel is additional credibility for your business case presentation.

WHAT DO I DO WHEN I AM IN A SALES SLUMP?

Bryan Flanagan, Sales Training, Flanagan Training Group

"There are two reasons sales professionals get into a sales slump, and there are two ways to get out of a sales slump. The first reason we get into sales slumps is that we've lost track of our basics. We have stopped doing the fundamental things that are necessary for success. The second reason is that we have lost our passion. We've lost sight of why we got into the world of sales in the first place. The cure: Return to the basics by asking questions and listening to the answers, soliciting referrals, and making calls. Also, find our motivation. Rekindle the fire we had in our bellies and in our hearts when we assist in making our clients better."

Bryan is right on many levels. Have you ever found yourself not in the mood to make another call or send another letter? My father had a saying for this: "Busy drives busy." What he meant was that if you do the right things to generate leads, other good leads will find a way to come to you. In Chapter 3, we discuss the need to call your existing customers to collect baseline data for your discovery questionnaire. This is a great first step in getting past a slump. Your customers will tell you how things are going for them, and you will be motivated by their successful use of your products. Discuss the value you have delivered and ask for referrals. (See Joanne Black's comment later in this chapter.) Talk to your prospects about other conversations (market research) you have had and successes that other customers have had using your product or parts of your product. Tell them about what is coming down the pike. You never know; they may order additional products or services. Do your homework on prospects in your pipeline, compare their metrics to the industry standards (Chapter 5), and call them to share your findings. Remember, get busy to stay busy and good things will come your way.

NOBODY CARES ABOUT YOUR PRODUCT, SERVICE, OR SOLUTION

Jill Konrath, author of *SNAP Selling* and *Selling to Big Companies*

> *"Your company is proud of its offering and wants you to tell the world*
> *how wonderful it is. But to your prospects, it's totally irrelevant.*
> *That's why they delete your messages in a nanosecond or refuse to set*
> *up meetings with you. Your prospects only care about achieving their*
> *objectives, getting their work done, and fighting the fires that pop up daily.*
> *To get on their calendar, focus on how you can have an impact on these*
> *areas. Let them know how you've helped other similar companies solve the*
> *same problems they face and the business results those companies have*
> *attained. You want to paint a stark contrast between their status quo*
> *and what's possible if they use your offering. But don't say a word about*
> *your leading-edge systems, unique methodologies, or passion for*
> *excellence. To beat the delete, it's all about the difference you can make*
> *for their business."*

Chapter 3 lays the foundation for understanding the fact that the status quo is not free. In Chapter 6, we teach you how to collect and present the information on why the status quo is not free. Jill makes an important point in that you must paint a stark contrast between the status quo and what is possible when a prospect purchases from you. The possibilities are defined by your already successful customers. Jill goes on to say, "It's all about the difference you can make for their business." A high-quality business case (Chapter 8) includes a section on the status quo and decision delay. In addition, we extrapolate cost over a three- to seven-year period (Chapters 3 and 8), so that you are able to have the threshold-for-pain discussion.

IT'S POSSIBLE TO ENTER THE BUYER'S JOURNEY EARLIER

Sharon Drew Morgan, author of *Dirty Little Secrets*

"After being very successful in sales, I founded a tech company and real-ized why buyers didn't buy the way I thought they should: Sales handles only the needs assessment/solution placement end of the buyer's decision, and ignores the private, political, relationship-based issues that must be resolved internally before a solution or a vendor can be considered. Unfortunately, this private process is not available to an outsider. Buying Facilitation® was developed as an add-on to sales, a change management model, similar to a coaching skill, to help buyers navigate through their unique, idiosyncratic decision-making/change-management process. Sellers do a great job of understanding pain, needs, and solutions, and can even be clever at strategizing. But this is all from the outside, and has no relevance to the fight that two department heads are having, or the old, beloved vendor that suddenly reappears. Every purchase is a change-management problem that cannot be resolved by sales, as sellers aren't privy to this activity. Buying Facilitation® can be easily added to the sales job to help manage the buying decision earlier in the journey."

In Chapter 4, we discuss the importance of research when determining whether a prospect is worth pursuing. Before you are able to interject your-self into the buyer's decision-making process, it is critical that you have an understanding of the prospect's strategic direction and ability to purchase from you. An annual report is a good source for familiarizing yourself with a company's inner workings. If the company is not publicly held and there is no annual report, use InsideView or Hoovers to do your homework. If all else fails, Google the company for a history of press reports.

Finally, for the referral to be successful for you, it is crucial that you understand your products and services and their impact on your prospect's financial statements (Chapter 3).

YOU CANNOT TEACH RAPPORT

Mike Bosworth, author, speaker, and entrepreneur

> *"I was led to believe that the only thing I could teach was process:
> strategies, tactics, and skills that would push a sale forward. Forming
> a connection was dependent on the inherent ability of the individual
> salesperson. I recognized the fact that people connect with and buy from
> those they trust. The two essential components of building trust, according
> to Stephen Covey, are sincerity and competence. For 32 years I had been
> teaching salespeople how to be competent, and the top-tier sellers, who
> connect intuitively, were able to get even better. For the bottom 87 percent,
> however, competence was not enough. They needed to learn to connect,
> and stories can build that connection.*
>
> *The fact is, leaders in virtually all professions are superb storytellers.
> Before the relatively recent invention of writing, our ancestors collected
> and passed down crucial tribal information through oral traditions.
> For the past one hundred and ninety thousand years, humans have used
> stories to communicate, educate, warn, persuade, engage, inspire, cele-
> brate, and connect emotionally. When a seller begins with some variety
> of 'I want to tell you a story . . . ,' the buyer's limbic brain creates an
> altered state of awareness. The left brain becomes relaxed and quieted for
> the imaginative right side. When immersed in a story, the buyer's brain
> is primed to visualize. The logical left brain is shut down and critical
> thinking is gone, setting the stage for the listener to be accepting of
> new ideas."*

I completely agree with Mike on the point that people like to buy from
people whom they trust and respect. However, learning to build rapport is
only a part of the success formula. Mike has taken a scientific approach to
teaching rapport by understanding what is occurring on the left and right
sides of the brain in a sales (social) situation.

Once again I agree with Mike that rapport is a critical first step in the
sales process. However, there are other attributes and skills required to take
advantage of the rapport-building process. For example, let's assume that

a sales professional approaches you to discuss a new product or service that he is offering, and let's say you feel an instant rapport with him. You like him. Now you begin to discuss the new product or service, and you quickly realize that this sales professional doesn't have any idea what this product does or what its impact on your business would be. The sales professional is just reciting the brochure or reading from a script. Credibility is gone! Is rapport still present?

The Key to the C-Suite is about knowing your product's value and its impact on your prospect's business (Chapter 3). Meeting C-level executives with knowledge in hand will increase your opportunity to build a solid relationship and help you build rapport initially and keep it going throughout the sales process.

BUYERS ARE LIARS, BUT THEN AGAIN, LIARS ARE BUYERS TOO

Ron Marks, author of *Managing for Sales Results*

"As I speak to audiences of salespeople, I often ask how many of them knew that they would be in sales when they were in high school. An astonishing majority got into sales by accident and received very little in formal sales training skills. I also never intended to get into sales. However, once I got out of school, I quickly realized that I was not going to be able to achieve my income goals in my original career path. I was fortunate to go to work at an early age for sales training legend Tom Hopkins, so I had a much greater opportunity to learn how to be a sales professional than most. However, no amount of study, classroom, or role-play experience prepared me for what I was going to encounter in the field of selling. Customers really don't like salespeople and are often dishonest in what they tell us.

Yes, I had heard the old saw that 'buyers are liars,' but I could not imagine that prospects would lie to me when I was trying to help them.

*What really frustrated me in the early days was how much time I wasted
creating proposals, making follow-up phone calls, and visiting prospects
who never intended to buy in the first place, yet did not have the courage
or consideration to tell me the truth in the beginning. I wasted so much
time in my first year getting the runaround. As a sales trainer today,
I try to help young salespeople understand the importance of thorough
questioning and establishing the proper expectations without creating a
negative impression of selling. I still believe, however, that most salespeople
just have to get knocked around a little in the first year. This is not
something that can simply be learned in school."*

Throughout this book, we try to make it clear how important it is to
do your homework. If you are able to use the tools you create to uncover
and identify pain, capture cost, and estimate your value, then you are
probably going to gain a better understanding of your prospect's ability to
purchase from you. In addition, as you submit confirmation letters to your
prospects, they must verify their pain and continue to engage you in the
sales process. Often prospects don't even realize that they are lying.
Responding to a sales professional's questions sometimes triggers a
defense mechanism in which they are giving you only enough information
to satisfy your question and get you to move on. The discovery process
(Chapter 3) is designed to ferret out inaccuracies and get to the heart of
the issue and the cost of the issue.

Let's face it, lying to you throughout the process serves no purpose if
a prospect wants honest feedback from the tools you have created. If a
prospect lies to you about your impact on her days' sales outstanding
(DSOs), why bother to participate in the process? When you are using sales
tools that identify pain, capture current and ongoing cost, calculate your
value, and determine financial impact (Chapter 7), it requires all parties to
be honest in their participation.

HOW DO YOU GET TO THE MEETING AT THE LEVEL THAT COUNTS?

Joanne S. Black, founder, No More Cold Calling

"Prospecting. That dreaded word for salespeople. To most, it means cold calling, sending direct mail, e-mailing, maybe even knocking on doors, and relying on social media to generate qualified leads.

The only smart prospecting strategy is referral selling. Why? Referral business closes a minimum 50 percent of the time. Plus, salespeople are presold, earn trust and credibility, shorten their sales process, incur no hard costs, and ace out the competition. No other marketing strategy comes close to these results. When companies use referrals, they increase their revenue and decrease their cost of sales.

A referral strategy is common sense, but not common practice—even among people who have been selling for years. Although sales executives and sales trainers tell us that we should ask for referrals, we never learned referral selling in school or in any sales training.

People are glad to introduce us to their contacts, but we must ask. Referral selling is simple and straightforward, and, when implemented, delivers sales prospects at the level that counts and converts prospects to new clients more than 50 percent of the time. If we don't get the meeting at the level that counts, nothing else matters. When we receive an introduction from a trusted referral source, we earn the right to have the meeting and conduct the subsequent ROI interaction. Why work any other way?"

Joanne's method of referral selling is tried and true. In addition to the success associated with referral selling, you also remove one of the biggest issues: the perceived risk of buying from you. Yes, as discussed in Chapter 5, risk mitigation is a critical success factor in selling to the C-Suite. However, if you approach a prospect that you were referred to, but you have little or no knowledge of its products, services, or management, then you are going to embarrass both yourself and the person who referred you. It is crucial that you do your homework before ever calling on a referral source. In Chapters 4 and 5, I provide you with several research resources. Chapter 5, in particular, explains where you can find the web site information from *Inc.* on industry norms for the C-Suite metrics. Remember, before you walk in the door, do your homework so that you can talk intelligently about the business, the market, and your value.

LEARN FROM THE BEST

Michael Norton, executive vice president of Global Accounts for Sandler Training, and chairman of the board and founder of www.candogo.com

> "*Mentorship is usually a best intention when it comes to training and teaching new sales professionals, but often it gets lost in the frenetic pace of just getting after the business. There is much to be learned from books and during role plays in the classroom; however, there is no substitute for seeing how the very best salespeople sell when they are live and in person with a real prospect or customer.*
>
> *A few years ago, I had the privilege of sitting with snowboard and skateboard champion Shaun White, AKA the Flying Tomato, on a flight from Minneapolis to Denver. Two of my children were competing on the Vail snowboard team that year, and I asked Shaun for just one thought or tip he could give me that might help make a difference in their performance. He told me that when he was young, he would follow his brother on the mountain everywhere he went. If his brother turned, he turned. If his brother jumped, he jumped. And, unfortunately, if his brother wiped out, Shaun was so close to him that he would run into him or wipe out, too. So his advice was simple yet profound: I should have my kids go into the terrain park and observe for a while, looking for the very best snowboarders on the hill that day. Then they should get in behind them and do what they do, even if it means wiping out a few times.*
>
> *Salespeople, especially new salespeople, should take the same advice. Don't wait for the company to implement a mentoring program; it may never really happen. Just seek out the very best salespeople on the team and ask to listen to calls, go on field visits, review proposals, and get involved in the deals and deal flow as they are happening. As Shaun White said to me, 'This alone will make a huge difference in their performance.'*"

The concepts contained in this book are not new to the world. Successful salespeople have been using these strategies for years. I met Tom Siebel once when I was consulting at a company in Chicago. Siebel flew in on his private jet, brought autographed copies of his books, and met with the CEO, CFO, and others (including me) to discuss using Salesforce.com. Tom was gregarious, humorous, and detailed; he knew the business, and he knew the impact that Salesforce.com would have on the company. I learned a lot that day just from observing Tom in action. Top executives use information to their advantage to persuade prospects to make decisions. They know their corporate value and its impact on the business, and they know how to articulate it to their prospects.

Michael's point of finding the best and shadowing their technique may not always be possible when it comes to selling to the C-Suite. However, the more opportunities you have to meet in the C-Suite, the better you become at communicating at this level.

LEARN HOW TO THINK LIKE A CHAMPION

Keith Rosen, global authority on sales leadership and author of the award-winning *Coaching Salespeople into Sales Champions*

> *"You've trained your salespeople on your product and service offerings, as well as the sales process you want them to follow every time they engage with a customer or prospect. They've all been trained on the same selling system. They've all been given the same tools and information. So, why aren't they all performing at the exact same level? After all, if success in selling is dependent only upon what you do or what process you follow, then each person on your team who is following the selling system should be performing at the same level. Regardless of industry or company, this is never the case. The fact is, when you look at any top performers and any great sales leaders, their success transcends simply what they do. In fact, it is more about who they are, how they communicate, and, most important, how they think that makes them truly great.*

Sales champions think differently. In essence, they are wired different-
ly from the average or below-average performer. That's why my formula
for success in selling isn't limited to activity and strategy, but instead, looks
more like this:

Consistent Execution + Proven Strategy (and the Right
Prospects) + Attitude/Characteristics (Confident, Best
Thinking, Enthusiastic, Creative, Resilient, Persistent, Driven,
Intuitive, Honorable, Seeks to Serve/Learn, Self-Aware,
Coachable, Etc.) + Best Practices/Skill Set + Company
(Product/Service, Etc.) + Communication Style = Success!

While each one of these variables is self-containing, they are collec-
tively dependent upon one another to achieve maximum productivity and
peak potential. That's why sales training alone is not enough. Salespeople
and managers can't always diagnose their own skill deficiencies, nor can
they coach themselves out of a slump. Managers focus on spreadsheets
and sales activity, and treat symptoms instead of the root cause, so similar
problems persist. Coaching moves beyond traditional training by fostering
best thinking, which develops true champions not only in form and style,
as in what they do, but, more important, in who they are and how they
think, which results in the acquisition and retention of more customers.
Beliefs precede experience, for it will always be the level of thinking you
embrace that shapes your outcome and results. If you focus only on the
strategic or doing side, then in essence, you're developing only half the
salesperson you can be. Think of the slogan for the U.S. Army, 'Be all you
can be.' It's certainly not, 'Do all you can do.'

It's one thing to look at a top performer and try to emulate what he
or she is doing. However, becoming a true champion yourself requires
looking under the hood and looking within others, as well as yourself,
to identify the characteristics and belief system that each sales leader
possesses. Successful people leverage a different model to achieve greater
results. They chose to maintain their level of self-worth by choice rather
than surrendering their personal power, allowing your experiences to
dictate how they feel about themselves.

They know never to allow external situations to dictate their internal
condition. They have discovered how to rise above the self-imposed

definition of who they think they are, often bounded by their past experiences. They have made their level of confidence unconditional by making it a choice. Ultimately, it will be the attitude and thinking that you choose to adopt as well as the limiting beliefs and assumptions that you choose to let go of that will become your driving force that fuels unprecedented success."

Keith points out what makes great sales professionals great: "It is more about *who* they are, *how* they communicate, and, most important, *how they think* that makes them truly great." A key to success in selling to the C-Suite is exactly this: *Who* you are, *how* you communicate, and *how you think*. In Chapter 2, where we have you build a value inventory, we ask that you "put yourself in your customer's shoes." This process will get you into the mindset of your prospect. Next, we discuss how to measure the threshold for pain. When you think like your prospect, pain measurement becomes much easier. You are likely to find and uncover hidden pain that the prospect wouldn't have mentioned in a normal sales situation.

Throughout the book, we discuss how to communicate your findings. We provide the vernacular that the C-Suite expects you to know (Chapter 1). We correlate your value with the financial impact that your customers care about most (Chapter 4). We discuss how to present your solution (Chapter 5), and how to build a financial dashboard (Chapter 6). Each chapter provides you with the tools that will make you unique in your discovery, presentation, and approach to communicating with the C-Suite.

CALL HIGHER OR DIE SLOWLY

Ken Edmundson, author of *Listen! You're Trying to Tell You Something* and *ShortTrack CEO*

> *"In today's environment, the best salespeople call on CEOs and presidents because presidents and CEOs don't have budgets—they make budgets.*

They don't ask other people what to do; they make decisions quickly. To connect with the president or CEO of a company, you need to present yourself as having equal business stature. You need to act and sell like a CEO. You need the following two mindsets to dominate your thoughts:

1. *I am the CEO of my business.*

2. *I absolutely believe that my product or service, along with my expertise, can make a difference in your business."*

CEOs depend heavily upon company financial information to make strategic buying decisions. In addition to the key information, they look at the value impact on a very select set of financial metrics—metrics like debt-to-equity ratio, return on assets, or earnings. These metrics signify how well the CEOs are doing in their job, sort of a CEO report card. The value of your products and services in relation to the financial impact on the CEO's key metrics is a primary determining factor in whether you will sell this opportunity or not. Knowing your value and its key impacts on the C-Suite metrics is also a key factor in your success. In Chapter 1 we laid out the vernacular, and in each chapter we discussed how you will use these metrics in the sales process to better communicate how you can have a positive impact on a prospect's financial situation.

Prior to your discussion with the CEO, read the company's annual report; gather personal information from InsideView, Jigsaw, or other sources; and have talking points ready for your meeting. Look up the industry norms for the C-Suite metrics as detailed on *Inc.*'s web site, and discuss the differences and impacts you may have on the company's strategic business objectives.

Ken is right when he says that CEOs don't have budgets, but they typically have someone to answer to. Shareholders, employees, and officers of the company all share a common goal, and the more you know about their business issues, pains, and goals, the more success you will have selling to them.

IT'S NOT ABOUT YOU

Michael Drake, founder/CEO, masterIT

> *"In our experience, we observe that salespeople often force all the features and benefits of their product or service on the prospect before ever really understanding (a) if there is a fit, (b) what the prospect's real pain is, and (c) the prospect's realization of the consequences of not fixing the problem. To uncover these three answers, salespeople must ask tough questions and then just listen. It is amazing what people will tell you if you are genuinely curious and will only ask."*

We began this book with an exercise to create a value inventory (Chapter 2). This process was designed to force your sales team to think like your customers. Use the knowledge of the market to drive your value. The process begins with putting yourself in your customers' shoes and asking, "Why would I buy a product or service like this one?" The final results from your value inventory will help you develop your discovery questions (Chapter 3). These questions are used to uncover pain and determine the current and ongoing cost of that pain. In addition, we discussed the threshold for pain. In other words, at what point will the prospects' pain reach a tipping point? When are they going to buy something to relieve themselves of the pain? This process is designed to get you to ask the right questions, listen to and document the answers, and provide your prospect with a roadmap to purchasing from you.

TARGET MARKETING IS A NECESSITY FOR SALES!

Steve Szamocki, general manager, GE Intelligent Solutions

> *"A valuable lesson that I learned over the years is the importance of solid market segmentation, buyer role identification, and pain sheet development. Companies will hire and terminate many salespeople because they are not as productive as they could be. If salespeople are*

to have a chance to succeed, however, 'marketing' needs to point them toward the right targets and arm them with the right buyer-influence value statements. The value statements or pain sheets not only need to include costs for the product or solution, but should also include tangible investment returns/payback."

Steve's point is very much in alignment with *The Key to the C-Suite*. In Chapter 5, we introduce you to a web site for comparing financial metrics like earnings before interest, taxes, depreciation, and amortization (EBITDA); net and gross profit margin; or debt-to-equity ratio within different vertical markets. Targeting a vertical market and knowing the norms for that market's financial metrics is an advantage that most sales professionals are not aware of. This information enables you not only to target the vertical market, but to pinpoint the areas of a prospect's financial statement where your solution will have the most impact. For example, if your product's value is in reducing labor cost, then your impact can affect earnings, net and gross profit margin, and operating costs. You can look at this web site to see where your prospect's normal operating range is for its particular vertical market and discuss how your impact will move it into or out of the normal range. This process works only if you understand your value and its effect on the C-Suite. This all starts in Chapter 2 with building your value inventory and proceeds throughout the book, where you will learn to build a high-quality business case.

YOU HAVE TWO EARS AND ONE MOUTH . . . USE THEM IN THAT PROPORTION

Charlie Gibbons, executive vice president for strategy, Wausau Financial; former marketing vice president at IBM

"We have been taught to 'talk with our customer.' What we have not been taught is to listen and what we should do before we ask the question. A number of years ago, it dawned on businesses that you should go out and talk to your customers to find out what they wanted. So everyone

reacted, and customers were deluged with, 'What do you want?' The problem is that customers look to us as the professionals for many of those answers. Often the customer does not really know what he wants. Customers get bogged down with their issues and business problems, and are often influenced by what others say is the problem. They cannot see the forest for the trees.

What we were taught is to always talk to our customer with the expectation that the customer is going to tell us what she needs, and that, if we respond, we will have a sale. Customers' reactions tend to be associated with the current issues they are dealing with or the latest problem, and they often do not have the insight and inside track that we were hoping to achieve. When you ask customers what it is that they need and they tell you and you tell them how you can fix it or how your product applies, you are reducing yourself to a commodity—you act and look just like your competitor.

Lee Iacocca, the former CEO of Chrysler, really had it right, in my opinion. He knew what others had not taught us. He knew to look and think first, then ask the customers and listen to what they said. He knew that customers assume that you are the expert in your area. So Iacocca instructed his people to fan out, go into parking lots, look into cars, and observe. Interestingly, they saw something that customers had just taken for granted—a mess! Then he sent his people out to talk with their customers. And they heard the same things that their competitors heard. However, his people would also ask about the mess they had seen, and offer suggestions such as, 'Would a cup holder help?' or, 'Would a trash basket be convenient?' The result was that Chrysler led the way with product innovation and creativity when it came to automotive conveniences, and competitors were forced to quickly follow suit. What Iacocca understood was that he had a responsibility not only to know his product, but also to have an understanding of the customer's environment. The result of his people taking the time to assess their customer's environment provided his people with ideas and opinions. One might conclude that his people were still essentially 'selling their products,' but he pushed the discussion from a commodity type of vendor to a value-added consultant.

Once you achieve that 'trusted advisor role' or 'consultative mantle,'
you are looked upon and treated differently, and your products take on
a different dimension. You are now perceived as valuable, and whether
your customers implement your ideas immediately or only consider them
for some time in the future, they will not dare to let you out of their
network because they will respect your ability and the potential risk of
missing a market shift."

Yogi Berra once said, "Baseball is 90 percent mental. The other half is physical." I am here to tell you, "Sales is 90 percent preparation. The other half is presentation." As stated in Chapter 2, it is crucial that you better understand how buyers buy. We tend to spend our money on teaching salespeople how to sell. The problem is that sales professionals need to make the adjustments on how to sell to a buyer that changes the way he buys, and are often reluctant to do so. Preparation for a sales call should include, at a minimum, a thorough understanding of your prospect's primary business. If it's a publicly held company, you should review its annual report; if not, Google it for news articles.

In addition, you need to be prepared to ask questions that help you identify pain that you can resolve, as outlined in Chapter 5. Listen to your prospect and think about what you learned when you created your value inventory. Remember, you are the one holding the key to understanding your value and its impact on the customer's financial metrics (Chapter 4). At the end of the day, if you are able to discuss your prospects' strategic goals and how your products or services will affect their financial well-being, then "they will not dare to let you out of their network."

SUMMARY

In Chapter 2, we asked the simple question, "Why do corporations spend millions of dollars teaching their sales professionals how to sell, yet very little is spent on helping them to understand why their customers buy?"

This book showed you how to get closer to buyers, earn their trust, build rapport, and gain a better understanding of how they make strategic buying decisions. Each concept is wrapped around the idea that your value has a financial impact on your prospect's business. That impact can be (and probably will be) measured on a regular basis. The insights from our contributors presented in this chapter provide us with some real-world experience on how, when, and where to use the concepts discussed in *The Key to the C-Suite.*

CHAPTER 10

ASSEMBLING THE PIECES

There are many pieces to developing your business case for the C-Suite. We started out in Chapter 2 by gaining a better understanding of your value when we created a value inventory. Next, we extended that value to determining the financial impact of your product or service on your prospect's business. This concept of building your value inventory resulted in a document that you can use to communicate with and sell to C-Suite executives, to teach new employees about your business, or perhaps as a foundation for developing your marketing plan. Creating your value inventory is one of those rare processes in which the steps you take to get to the end result are as valuable as the output. Bringing your team together to build this document is a great learning experience and bonding exercise, and it provides a valuable lesson in understanding your value proposition and how it affects your potential customers.

Next, we helped you design a primary discovery-questionnaire document that is useful for identifying a prospect's issues, pains, and goals. The questions you formulated were all quantitative-based questions, designed to identify an issue, capture and calculate the current cost of that issue, and provide the ability to extrapolate that cost over a period of years. The questions should be grouped by issue. For example, all labor-based questions should be in one section, inventory questions in another, and reporting questions in another. Each section may include cost reductions, revenue increases, or cost avoidances. These groups or categories are part of the foundation for building a business case that is easy for you to explain and just as easy for your prospect to understand.

Once you developed the questions for your primary discovery tool, we added a concept called "value estimation." This is the point in the sales process where you want to establish goals that your prospect can achieve by using your products or services. We suggested that you use social proof (customer testimonials, surveys, or site visits) to determine what your average customer has gained by using your products or services. In addition, we discussed the use of outside research from consulting firms like Gartner Group or PricewaterhouseCoopers.

Dashboard development was the next concept that we discussed. Dashboards are used to assimilate the data you collected using the primary discovery and value estimation documents. We helped you design a financial dashboard that you can use in the sales process to input the status quo and receive feedback on the impact that your products or services may have on your prospect's financial metrics. Dashboard design is linked directly to the development of your business case document.

We discussed the use of financial metrics when developing your financial dashboard, metrics such as days' sales outstanding (DSOs), return on assets (ROA), return on equity (ROE), or debt-to-equity ratio, which are used by C-Suite executives to make strategic buying decisions. As part of the process of building your value inventory, we had you define which metrics your products or services affect the most. The result of this effort is built into the financial dashboard, so that you are able to compare your prospect's current situation to the future impact, based on estimated value delivered. This C-Suite effect is one of the highlights of a high-quality business case. Keep in mind that you can compare the results to industry norms, as discussed in Chapter 5.

The business case document is the final result of all the data collection, goal setting, and status quo establishment. We had you collect the data and parse it so that your prospect could recognize all the time, effort, and analysis that went into the creation of the document. There are several sections spread out across several pages that are designed to include the data, charts, and graphs that allow for an easier understanding of the issues defined, the current and ongoing costs, and the goals established. The business case is the document you will use to close the deal.

Precall planning is a key component of success when selling into the C-Suite. Be sure to do your homework. Read your prospects' annual report and 10-K. Lead a discussion on C-Suite impact and identify the metrics that are most important to your prospect. Use outside resources like Jigsaw, Hoovers, or InsideView prior to a call on the C-Suite.

ROADMAP TO THE C-SUITE

- Develop a value inventory.
  - Determine why your customers buy.
  - Capture business issues, pains, and goals.
  - Identify stakeholders.
  - Include your solution and the value you provide.
  - Use your in-house CFO to help with the C-Suite effect.
- Create primary discovery questions.
  - Identify pain.
  - Establish the status quo.
  - Extrapolate the cost (pain) over three to seven years.
    - Determine the threshold for pain.

- Create output reports for customer review and confirmation.
- Use research for proof of estimated value delivered.
  - Use social proof.
    - Survey your current customers.
    - Determine value goals for three to seven years.
- Create a financial dashboard.
  - Compartmentalize the data collected.
  - Summarize the data collected.
  - Create detail sections for the data collected.
    - First-year cost and value
    - Multiple-year cost and value
    - Investment summary
    - Cost of the status quo
    - Impact on C-Suite metrics
    - Cash flow analysis
  - Include industry norms for comparison.
- Create your business case document.
  - Use dashboard data for baseline.
  - Add graphics.

Use this checklist to track your progress when selling to the C-Suite. Be sure to complete each step, and try not to skip ahead. Remember, the journey to building your business case is as valuable as the business case itself.

INDEX